The Competency Question and Answer Book

Mike Good

To my mother,
to whom I owe everything

Createspace Publishing

CONTENTS

Chapter 1   What is a competency ?

1.1   Competence

A **competency** is simply a skill or an ability to do something efficiently. Giving good service to a customer is a competency. Showing attention to detail is another.

Years ago, interviewers used to ask candidates a whole range of questions such as "*What have you done in the past ? *" *"Why do you want to work for us ?" " What school did you attend ? " " What qualifications do you have ?"*

 Later,   there was a fashion for ' situational interviewing ', in which candidates would be told a situation and then told to *imagine* how they would react to it. An example that you might have been given is "*Imagine that you are working in an office and you receive a phone call in which the caller tells you that there is a bomb in your building . How would you react to it ? " *   Or : *"Imagine that one of your work colleagues tells you that he fiddles his expenses account. What would you do ?"*

Nowadays, interviewers have moved away from that type of interviewing after psychologists told them that competency interviewing -(which is also known as ' behavioural based interviewing ') - is a better guide to how we would perform in any job. It is believed that our past behaviour is a much more accurate guide to our future behaviour and therefore many more companies have now adopted the competency approach.

1.2   How competency interviews work

In a competency interview, you will be asked about your experiences. **You will be asked to provide examples of how you performed particular tasks**. So, if the job involves working with customers in any way, you could be asked to give an example of how you have delivered excellent customer satisfaction ; or perhaps how you have dealt with an irate or demanding customer. If the job involves cash-handling, you might well be asked to give an example of when you have demonstrated attention to detail.
Most current interviews last between 25 and 45 minutes and typically you can expect to be asked about **four or five** competency questions by a couple of interviewers. Each question will invite you to give an example of **how** you have used that skill in the past and each answer should last about 3 minutes.   You must answer in a certain way : you must describe a particular situation or problem that needed resolving, the action you took to resolve it and what the outcome and benefits were.

4

1.3   The advantages to you of competency interviews

In a later chapter, I shall be showing you how it is possible to predict some of the probable questions in the interview. So, one advantage is that you can **prepare your answers in advance**. Many people hated the old situational interviews, where you were suddenly given a hypothetical scenario and asked to imagine what you would do .Often, jobseekers had never encountered that situation before in their lives and the experience was really stressful. Thankfully, those types of interviews are rare now. As well as being able to prepare your answers, you can **practise them** over and over again.

These interviews give you the opportunity to really sell your talents and your worth to an employer. If you have actually done the job or done the task that you are being asked about, then the employer is often **willing to overlook any lack of qualifications** that you may have. Employers are now more interested in what you have <u>done</u>, not who you are or how much you have managed to memorise .

Another great advantage is that, unless the interviewer specifically asks you for an example from work, you can relate **an example from any sphere of your life**. It might be a group you are involved in or some voluntary work you once did or some experience you once had while on holiday. This is very important and I shall be saying a lot more about this in the next chapter.

So, to those who dread competency interviews, I say : ' Have no fear ! 'From now on, I want you to change your mindset and to see them in a totally different light. You must see them as glorious opportunities. If you follow the guidelines and are willing to work hard, you will be in a much better position and actually look forward to showcasing your skills at such interviews !

Advantages of competency based interviews to jobseeker :

- •   You can predict some of the questions and therefore prepare for them
- •   You can practise your answers
- •   You can sell your talents and worth , even if you may not have the required qualifications
- •   You can use examples from outside of work

1.4   Competency based application forms

These too are becoming more common and more employers are using them as a way of sifting out candidates. Sometimes, literally hundreds of people apply for just a handful of jobs. Naturally, they cannot all be invited for an interview and increasingly employers are using this method to determine which applicants can demonstrate that they already have the required skills. It saves the employer expensive training costs.

These competency questions on applications forms are an excellent opportunity to sell yourself and to convince the employer that you are the solution to his business needs. Moreover, you are not under the pressure of an interview when completing the form. You can do it at your leisure. From now on, I want you to be positive about these type of application forms because we will now be examining how we can much more easily complete them once you have built up our personal experience autobiography.

Occasionally, the application process will involve selecting answers from given Competency Options . I will deal with this in Chapter 11.

Chapter 2   Doing an experience stocktake

2.1   The experience stocktake

One of the greatest difficulties that jobseekers face at competency interviews is that they cannot think of a specific occasion of when they have performed that competency and cannot describe an example to demonstrate their skills in that area. It is highly frustrating for them because they know that they have carried out that action many times to a high standard before but cannot recall it on demand. They lose the job of their dreams. Is this you ?

To pre-empt this happening to you as much as you possibly can, you must make yourself aware of all the experiences you have had. To do this, I am going to get you to realise and recognise that you employ many more skills than you may realise. I want you to do **an experience stocktake**.

Sofia worked in a call-centre. I asked her to list her duties. She replied: " *I answered incoming calls from people who had seen ads in papers, took their details and arranged for info to be sent out* ".

Actually, what she did was to deliver excellent customer service in a friendly and professional manner by taking incoming calls . She would use her great communication skills to actively listen and communicate appropriately and sometimes employ her persuasion and business acumen skills to sell additional items. She would use her time management skills to control talkative callers and meet her targets and her negotiation skills and problem-solving skills to sort out any callers who phoned in with complaints. She often exchanged her shift days with colleagues, showing her teamwork nature. She would log the confidential details of callers onto the inhouse software , while still actively listening, demonstrating her multi-tasking ability and IT skills.

Can you see that while Sofia thought that she only answered calls took details and arranged for items to go out, she actually has a broad range of skills that she can use as starting points for examples in an interview situation ? This is so typical. Most people do not realise that they have many skills until they are pointed out to them or are forced to sit and evaluate themselves.

2.2   List your duties in detail

Now comes the hard work. This chapter demands a great deal of work from you but I make no apology for that. Nothing in life is free. The rewards will be worth it.

If you are currently working, I want you to list what you did in your job last week, **in detail.** Every duty you had to perform, no matter how small or trivial it may seem. If last week was not a typical week because you were on a training course for example, then use a typical week. List all the people you liaised with, both inside your workplace and outside. List any incidents . List all the equipment / machinery you used. That is very important. List every function you performed, even the smallest.

Why ? Because every experience you have had could help you to land that job you seek. The purpose of this is to get you to ultimately see that **you have many more abilities than you realise** and have had many more experiences than you think.

Let me explain. Josh was an office worker and wondered at first why I was asking him to list the office machinery he used. It then prompted him to remember that the fax/ photocopier had a paperjam last week. That in turn reminded him about the time last year when he was alone because everyone was out to lunch and the fax/photocopier had jammed and he had a really urgent fax to send and how he was in a real mess. He decided not to panic.
He stayed calm and considered all his options. He thought about it for a few moments. He remembered that there was a manual in the fax drawer. He looked and found it wasn't there. He stayed calm and thought again. He copied down the name and model number of the machine, searched for it in Google, found the manual online, followed the trouble-shooting diagrams and quickly found the solution. So, he then realised that he did have problem-solving skills after all and had an example that he could use in any competency interview. He could also use that experience as an ' Initiative' example.

You must understand that all our experiences in life are important and that we forget most of them. Your task over the coming days and weeks is to try to remember those experiences and list them. From now on, you must get into the habit of recording your experiences in your **Experiences Autobiography**. More about that later .

So, list every function that you performed last week in your job.

- Whom did you communicate / meet with ? Inside or outside the job.

- Did you work with others in any way ? Teamwork skills ?

- Did you perform a service of any kind whatsoever ?

- Did you have any sort of deadlines or targets to meet ? daily ? monthly ?

- Did you achieve anything ?

- Did you solve any problems ? not a single one ?

8

- Did you organise anything ?
- Did you create anything ?
- Did you manage anything ? Did you improve, innovate, suggest something ?
- Did you show flexibility ?   Adapt to new changes / new working practices ?
- Overcome setbacks or obstacles ?
- Did you negotiate ? Did you persuade ?
- Make major decisions ?
- Plan something ?   Take responsibility for something ?
- Give a presentation ?
- Take the initiative ?
- Motivate someone ?
- Save the company any money or save waste ?
- Use ANY equipment ?

Think very slowly and carefully and take your time. This exercise must not be rushed or omitted.   Don't be lazy. Invest time in this and you will be very surprised at what you find. A small experience can often spark a memory of something which can give you an excellent competency example for your interview.

If you do not have a job at the moment, then list all the things you did in your last two jobs.
Remember to write down even the smallest thing you did. All the people you spoke to, inside and outside the company. All the equipment you used. All the incidents.

If you are a school-leaver or have never worked, no problem ! This next part applies to you too.

2.3 Now list every job you have ever done

Now comes the really hard work ! I want you to do the same for **all your previous** jobs. Yes, that's right, every single one. Seriously. Even if all your previous jobs have been in the same line of work, there will have been

9

incidents that provide examples that can be used in your interview. The challenge now is for you to dig through your memory and exhume those long forgotten experiences and achievements. They can prove to be very valuable. The more time and effort you invest in remembering your past experiences, the far easier it will be to demonstrate your skills to an employer and land that dream job. It's that simple.

Ask your family and friends for help !   Ask you family, friends, partner, relatives and colleagues to remind you of all your previous jobs and things that have happened to you in the past. Log them all. For now, in no particular order.

2.4   List any of these achievements or activities :

School - Attended all year round - you never missed a day ? Head boy ? One of the house captains ? Any special responsibility ? In drama society ? In debating team ? In choir ? Best achiever of the Year ? Won the cross country county race ? Team sports captain ? It's unlikely that you would be asked to prove these by the interviewer but it will show the interviewer what type of person you are, what you achieved and can form the basis of other examples. Even being in the choir shows you can work in a team.

Scouts / Girl Guides / St John's Ambulance Brigade -Any notable achievements ? Raised any money for charity ? Saved a life ?

Part-time jobs while at school   Paper boy. Milk boy. Cleaner. Saturday job helping in a shop, yard, garage, market stall or farm. Note : no job is worthless. Every job is useful and has dignity and value, if done well, even the most humble.

Voluntary work or charity work   -   Did you shop for the elderly ? Decorated an old folks' flat ? Mowed their garden lawn ? Shovelled their snow away ? Raised money ? Looked after a pet ? Did a charity sponsored run/ marathon /walk ? Served in a second-hand shop ? Acted as a delivery driver for a charity shop ?   Drive anyone home ? Served meals to the homeless at Christmas ? Handed out food at a food bank ? Organise a food bank ?

Community work   Organised a fireworks party for your street ? Organised or helped to run any sort of community party / celebration / commemoration for your block of flats, street or community ? Acted as chairman, treasurer, minutes-taker or in any capacity in any neighbourhood watch / security scheme ? Act as a local spokesperson or representative ?

10

Church work Have assisted in any way at your local church ? Helped organise or run annual fete ? Helped run the food bank ? Visited the elderly or sick ?

Local sports club Washed their kit ? Designed their leaflets ? Coached the kids ? Raised money for them ? Organised raffles bingos for them ? Worked in a team to clear snow off the pitch ?

Neighbours Solved disputes between them ? Done favours for them ? Communicated on their behalf ? Worked as a team with them ? Organised a street party or fireworks party ?

Local hospital - Ever helped them ? Attended their fete ? What happened ? Ever been a patient ? Made arrangements ? Visit the sick as a volunteer visitor ?

Local old cinema / concert hall - Ever tried to save it from closure ?

Olympic torch - Did you carry it ? What happened ?

In a hobbies club : chess, gardening. reading, inventing, computing, archery, cooking ? What happened ? Did you organise any competitions ? work as teams ? any accidents happen ? Resolve any problems or disputes ?

Travel experiences - see a crime ? negotiate a better deal ? have to change to a different hotel or airport ? get lost ? miss a flight ? give English lessons for free board or food ? prevent an accident ? had to hitch-hike ? get mugged or held up at gun-point ?

Health club / Gym Motivated yourself ? Lost weight ?

Evening-classes Taken courses to improve your skills ?

Driving test - any incidents ? make any sacrifices to pay for your lessons ?

Wedding - best man duties ? Had to give a speech ?

Holidays - planned any ? organised any ?

Family jobs with your children or nephews / nieces / grandchildren - Things you've done with kids : Organised birthday parties. Organised days out.

Any internships, work experience, placements, training courses, job-shadowing, school / uni coursework ?

Dig out all your old payslips and diaries to remind you of your previous jobs. Find all certificates of achievements, accolades, awards, letters of promotion and qualifications. All of these are vital reminders of your experiences and skills.

A warning. If you have already compiled a CV, don't be tempted to think that your CV is sufficient and that you can omit the above exercise. A CV is merely a brief skeleton of your past. I want you to spend a good deal of time painstakingly reminding yourself of every single task you have ever done. If it takes you a week, then so be it. I cannot emphasise enough the importance of this exercise.

2.5   Building your Experiences Autobiography

The next step is to buy an A4 pad and a hard folder for it. On the front of the folder, write in a permanent black pen ' **Experiences Autobiography** '. .Alternatively, if you can afford to buy a large hardback notebook, whose pages have already been subdivided from A to Z, then so much the better.

The task now is to transfer your past experiences into your Experiences Autobiography by categorising them in a way which will assist you in getting your next job.

At the top of the page of your A4 pad, write the following competencies, one on each sheet :

- Adaptability to Change - Flexibility, Versatility
- Attention to Detail - Accuracy
- Communication Skills - Verbal or written . Phone Skills.
- Customer Service   - Internal and external
- Deadlines, Targets and Achieving incl. Time Management
- Decision Making and Problem Solving
- Drive, Determination and Resilience, incl. self-motivation
- Initiative
- Negotiation, Persuasion , Influence and Motivating others
- Teamwork

You should have a separate sheet for each competency.

If you are using an A-Z notebook, obviously, you would enter *Teamwork* under T, both *Customer Service* and *Communication* under C (a separate page), *Decision Making* under D ,etc.

2.6   Logging your experiences into competencies

So, here is an example of how you must log all your past experiences into your Experience Autobiography file or book. Peter is an 18 year-old school-leaver who has not worked full-time but has remembered that he worked as a paper-boy and on one occasion, he noticed a man lying on the floor in his hallway.
He looked through the letter-box and realised that something was seriously wrong, went to the next-door neighbour and had him call an ambulance. His quick thinking saved that man's life. So, under the competency sheet headed ' *Initiative*', he writes ' Paperboy job - incident'. That will remind him of that situation. While he was doing that job, he also had to interact with his customers, so he writes ' Paperboy job ' on his ' *Customer Service* ' sheet. Same again for ' *Communication* ' sheet.

When he was in the 6th form, he was part of a group that were given a day's instruction in decorating and then volunteered to decorate a pensioner's flat. They had to complete it in four days. So, he wrote ' Decorated pensioner's flat ' under the following competency categories : *Deadlines, Targets and Achieving; Attention to Detail, Teamwork*. That one experience can serve him for 3 competency examples.

John is 19. He has had one part-time job and one full-time job. When at school, he had a Saturday job washing cars. It did not involve meeting the customers but he did have to wash so many cars per hour and to a high standard. So, he writes Washed Cars under the competency category *Deadlines, Targets and Achieving* and also again under *Attention to Detail*. He had a full-time temporary job as a Mailroom Assistant in a team with an Insurance Company. So, he enters 'Mailroom Assistant ' under the *Teamwork* ' category. He remembers that the job involved carefully weighing the post and calculating the correct postage of envelopes and packages. So, he enters Mailroom Assistant Weighing under ' *Attention to Detail* '. He remembers that he had to liaise with the staff on all floors, taking their instructions and also receiving post from couriers . He enters 'Mailroom Liaison with staff and couriers' under the *Communication* competency. Since he had strict time deadlines each day to meet , he notes that under the *Deadlines, Targets and Achieving* competency.
Finally, since the job had its ups and downs in volumes of work due to mailshots , TV ads, etc, he had to be flexible over shifts, staying late and working overtime. He writes ' Required overtime at Mail job' under the *Change, Flexibility and Adaptability* category.

2.7   Do you get the idea ?

If John now applies for a job which has a competency interview and the interviewer asks him for examples of when he has ever had to pay attention to detail or work in a team or communicate with others or work to a deadline or be flexible at work, he has ready- made examples in his Experiences Autobiography. .

He has these examples **because he has taken the time and trouble** to think exactly and specifically of the actions he has done in the past, to write them down and then to assign them to one or more competencies. That is your challenge. The reward is a good job. Now do it !

2.8   If you are returning to work after a long time away from the workplace

If you are perhaps a parent or a carer who has been at home for some years and   are now trying to get back into the world of work which is different from the equally demanding world of housework and caring, you will need to give employers examples of your behaviours which meet the required competencies.

Although returning to work can seem daunting, don't worry : millions have achieved it and so can you. Firstly, most employers are equally accepting of examples from outside the workplace. Secondly, you can easily build up a strong Experiences Autobiography with valid , excellent examples of your competence and skills by realising that what you have done in the home and with others are " transferable skills" . All you need is to get into the habit of closely identifying your actions.

For example, if you are asked in an interview for an example of how you have **organised**, you can state how you have organised your child's birthday party or playgroups or arranged babysitters or planned ahead for your child's new term. You have organised your time effectively so that all the washing, cleaning, ironing, shopping, school runs, visits to doctors and chemists and all meals are prepared on times and kids are bathed all on time . You know how much organising that takes and don't let others underestimate it.

If asked for an example of your **attention to detail,** you would tell of how you got all your kids to school on time each day, how you budgeted perfectly and how you paid all your bills perfectly without incurring any penalties. You budgeted ahead for birthdays, bills and emergencies too.

For examples of **flexibility and versatility**, you often had to adapt to unexpected circumstances, such as when your kids became ill, were sent home from school (teachers on strike, school snowed off,),your kids had accidents and you found a solution to the problem.

Communication skills ?You have had to deal with the teachers and PTA, the council, the Benefits Agency . You can mention the other groups you may be part of, including online forums.

Determination and resilience ?   Describe how you stuck up for your child's rights through thick and thin in a prolonged struggle with the Education Department or school or how you won a long benefit claim for the person for whom you were caring.

14

You will need to persuade prospective employers that the life skills you have developed over the years – and they are indeed valuable and considerable - are relevant to them and to the advertised job.

To do this, you will need to examine every single action you have taken while you have been out of the workplace. Yes, I know it is a laborious job but nothing comes easy to us in life and you will ultimately be rewarded if you do so. Write all your experiences into your **Experiences Autobiography**, as I have described.

2.9   If you are a young person with very little work experience

Don't despair. The same applies to you as to the members of the group in 2.8   You too can build up an Experiences Autobiography by relating all your school experiences and all the experiences with friends, on holidays in various groups and in the community – even in online groups and friendships – as examples of your skills.
You can even use experiences with your family members or friends. These are just as valid.

For example, when asked for examples of **Adapting to Change,** you can say how you adapted to a new home / teacher /6th form/ step-parent/ baby sibling/ the loss of someone or any sudden change, welcome or otherwise.

Attention to Detail – Any Maths, Science or Computing students should have no difficulty narrating how their equations or formulae had to be exact, to balance or how their computer program they had coded had to be without a single error in order to run.

For **Communication** examples, you can state you can state how you read books on essay-writing technique : the need to plan it, to have a brief intro of a couple of sentences, a main body of two or three paragraphs where it develops and then a final paragraph where you summarise it all and perhaps state your conclusion. You might remember how you had to give a small speech or presentation to your class on your coursework or how you explained the internet or mobile phones or Skype to elderly people.

For **Customer Service,** you might give examples from your Saturday job (include the training you were given for it) in a shop or on your uncle's market-stall or the times you served at your school fetes.

For examples of working to **Deadlines and Targets**, you might care to mention how you prioritised your assignments / essays/ coursework and exam preparation by deciding what was Urgent, what was Important and which was Non-urgent and allowing Contingency Time for any emergencies. Note the specific examples and of how you organised things.

For **Decision Making**, stick with how you went about selecting your options or choosing your college or uni. State how you went about your decision. You'll find this in Chapter 7.6.

For **Drive, Determination and Resilience,** maybe you passed your exams after recovering from a bad accident or a family bereavement or divorce. Maybe you lost weight or eventually managed to run a half-marathon or ride 40 miles on your bike after several attempts. The point is that you persevered and didn't give up. Show them that.

For **Teamworking** examples, you can narrate how you participated in a team project, perhaps how you contributed computer code or some ideas. Remember that you can use any experiences from outside of school, so tell of how you help the neighbourhood / community team clear up litter from the street / park / woods. Perhaps you played in a team, even an online one. That is valid too.

A prospective employer is willing to accept all and any of your examples , if they are well prepared and you can show him that your past behaviour matches what he is looking for.   Believe me, you can do it. Many have done it with my help and YOU can too.

Chapter 3 How to predict the competencies you might be asked

Okay, you've been called for an interview and you know or suspect that it will consist of competency questions. Your task now is to predict which competencies you will be tested on as best as you can and to prepare your answers for them as best you can.

3.1 Deconstructing the job advert

How is it possible to predict the competencies ? There is , of course, no absolutely certain way of knowing in advance what you will be asked - but employers are very busy people , who don't waste their time. **They will ask you about the competencies which are directly relevant to the job** for which you are applying and these are contained in the job advert and in the job description. More information may be available on the company website about the competencies needed or in any application pack or supplementary guidance notes sent to you. The biggest clues will come from the job advert itself and it is **by close analysis and deconstruction of the job advert** that we will be able to predict the likely questions that the interviewers will ask.

Let us examine a real job advert :

Example A

Customer Service Adviser , South East London, £ 8.50 per hour
As a Customer Service Advisor you will be responsible for the first line and follow up customer contacts by dealing with a mixture of inbound and outbound contacts, taking calls, writing letters and emails and assisting in projects to continuously improve our customer services.

Duties include: Respond to customer enquiries in warm, friendly and personable tone ---- Deal with customer complaints ---Log calls on to the PC ----Provide customers with product and service information ---- Report and escalate any priority issues ----Recognise and use opportunities to promote other services-----Administration : Write clear, concise and customer focused letters and emails.

Skills and Knowledge:

Excellent written and verbal communications skills are essential---Must have previous work experience within a customer services environment

-----Experience of multi-tasking (simultaneously using the telephone and PC based applications) preferred

The idea now is to carefully scrutinize the advert and to identify which competencies the interviewer is demanding. Read the advert carefully. Try to get a feel for the job. What will the worker be doing all day long ?

Having read the job advert, do you think the interviewer will ask us about *Project Management* skills ? Absolutely not. It is not that kind of job and there is no mention of that. *Leadership* skills ? Again, highly unlikely because nothing is mentioned in the advert about leadership. We must focus on which skills are being sought or implied

We need to write down the required competencies. The title of the job is sometimes a real help and in this case, it is a real giveaway. So, taking a new sheet of paper, we write <u>Customer Service</u>. Next, it says ' *dealing with inbound contacts* ' and *writing letters and emails* ', so we write down ' <u>Communication</u> '.
'*Respond to customer enquiries*' and *'Deal with customer complaints* ' is already is covered by Customer Service. It says ' *Log calls on to the PC'*, so we write <u>Attention to Detail</u> . We see *'Recognise and see opportunities to promote other services'* and so write <u>Negotiation and Persuasion</u> . Administration ? We have already covered this in Communication.

It says that written and communication skills are **'essential'**. This is a **major clue** in predicting what questions will be asked in a competency interview. Whenever the job advert or any job description states the word 'essential' or it says ' **must have'**, then it is almost guaranteed that you will be asked to give an example of that.

Here, it also says 'must have' previous experience in a customer services environment. It asks for multi-tasking, so we write <u>Change. Flexibility, Adaptability</u> .

3.2   Prioritizing the competencies

We have noted five competencies but we now prioritize them . We look to see which of those were demanded as ' **essential** ' or ' **must have** ' qualities. They were *Communication Skills* and *Customer Service* Skills. It is a <u>certainty</u> that these will be asked at the interview and a high probability that the other three will be the other questions at the interview. On average, interviewers ask four or five competency questions. In later chapters we look at the potential questions in greater detail and how to answer them.

18

Occasionally, employers will also use words such as **imperative, vital, key ,
paramount, critical or crucial.** If any of these appear, treat them as '
essential ' competencies and expect to be asked about them at the
interview.

Let us examine now another job advert :

Example B

*Meter Reader South West London 37 hours per week - flexible working
between 8am-8 pm Weekly Pay £281 plus up to £100 bonus and
additional mileage allowance*

The role :

* *Working with XXXX, you will represent many of the UK's leading
energy providers, visiting a wide variety of customers at their homes*

* *You will work within 30 mile radius of your home address and
mileage is fully expensed from the moment you leave your house.*

* *Visiting people at their homes you will be reading their gas and
electricity meters. completing visual safety checks and accurately recording
your readings onto a handheld terminal*

* *The ability to plan your own route and manage your diary and
workload to achieve the targets set for that day/week is essential*

*Must have had some previous customer service experience. If you are self
motivated and would be committed to this long term opportunity and a
resident of the SW postcode, please apply by sending your CV to YYY.*

Read it carefully. From the first bullet point, we might guess that <u>Customer
Service</u> might be asked. The second bullet point gives us no clues. The third
definitely confirms our suspicions about experience of Customer Service
and also the necessity for experience of <u>Attention to Detail</u>. The final bullet
point tells us that the competencies of <u>Time Management and Targets</u>
achieving will be required. The last paragraph tells us that Customer
Service is demanded , as is self-motivation, so we note <u>Self-Motivation</u> too.

What do you do now ? You prioritize by going back and looking for those
all important words .. ... ' **essential** ' and **'must have.'**

In the above example, the employer used 'essential ' in the fourth bullet
point, so we can expect the employer to focus on the candidate's diary

management skills and his ability to achieve his targets. The advert also stressed that customer service was 'essential', so the candidate must focus on preparing good examples of when he has provided excellent customer service in the past , as he will certainly be asked to do so in the interview. No doubt about it. He must also prepare good examples of his attention to detail and motivation but these do not seem to be as important to the employer.

Example C   *Role: Prisoner Custody Officer*

Hours: 40 during training and then 35 hours per week when fully trained

We currently require Prison Custody Officers working 35 hours per week on various shifts. Your role as a Prisoner Custody Officer is to provide a safe and secure environment for people committed into custody by the courts. A Prisoner Custody Officer supervises and manages prisoners, promotes good behaviour, ensures that all rules, orders and instructions are followed to ensure those in our care are treated with dignity and respect whilst maintaining safety and security.

Previous experience is not essential as full training will be provided. To secure one of these demanding but rewarding roles you will need to be able to demonstrate first class communication skills, the ability to write concise but accurate and clear reports, be committed to team work and have the awareness to ensure security is maintained at all times.

Main Duties:

* *Ensure the security and welfare of those in our care is maintained at all times*

* *Ensure all incidents are reported and dealt with effectively, including assaults, substance misuse and self harm*

* *Uphold respect for Prisoners, their property, rights and dignity*

Essential Skills and Experience:

* *Ability to work as part of a team*

* *Ability to report accurately both verbally and in writing*

* *Excellent communication skills*

* *Ability to handle stressful situations*

20

Read the above job advert carefully and list the competencies that the employer would most likely demand.

The ad says that previous experience of maintaining safety and security is **not** essential. What **is** essential and what I hope you have noted down are the following :

Teamwork , Communication skills and Customer Service Skills. Although 'Customer Service ' has not been explicitly stated, you would be dealing with other people and so this is implied and to be expected. The ability to write clear, concise and accurate reports is demanded. Also, in the first paragraph, did you notice that it says : A Prison Custody Officer .. promotes good behaviour' ? This to me indicates that they are looking for someone who has good negotiating skills. Someone who can persuade disruptive or upset prisoners to calm down . It is reinforced by the last line in Essential Skills... ' The ability to handle stressful situations ' That, of course is advanced interpersonal behaviour, which comes under good Communication Skills but also under Negotiation and Persuasion. People with high Negotiation and Persuasion skills can quickly get themselves out of stressful situations.

I would suggest that ' promotes good behaviour' might easily have been missed if you had read the advert in a perfunctory manner. It is imperative that you **analyse job descriptions very carefully**, word by word and read between the lines.

Ask yourself; Which four or five competencies, **according to this advert**, am I **most** likely to be asked ? Then ask yourself, which are the most likely **two or three** ?

3.3 Summary   You should now understand how to analyse job adverts to predict which competencies are required.

- Read the advert several times.

- Read it **word for word.**

- Remember to read any other job-description or material that came in the job-pack and anything on the company website which may give clues.

- Sometimes competencies are explicitly stated, sometimes not.

- Prioritize those marked as **essential**, or ' **must have** ' or similarly described. You **will** be questioned on them.

21

Chapter 4 How to predict the interview questions

4.1 Predicting the questions

Although it is not possible to predict all the questions you might be asked, it is possible to predict a good deal of them. If you have narrowed down the required competencies , as outlined in the previous chapter, you are homing in on the action. No two jobs are exactly alike and no two companies are exactly alike so it is impossible to be definitive. Once again, we must return to the actual job advert and give it a close reading. Let us return to Example A from Chapter 3 again. We decided that **Customer Service** and **Communication** were the two most important competencies demanded.

4.2 The most frequently asked questions on **Customer Service** are :
Tell me of a time when you have :

1.   Given great customer service / Gone the extra mile for a customer.

2.   Dealt with a difficult customer / Handled a complaint.

3.   Failed to deal with an awkward customer.

Examining the advert, we see that we are expected to respond to enquiries in a friendly manner and provide product information. So, we can predict that we shall be asked question 1.... given good customer service. You will need to look through your Experiences Autobiography for an example of such an occasion.

Since the ad clearly says you will be handling complaints, we can predict that you could be asked question 2 ...handled a complaint. You will need an example of when you have done this.

Interviewers often ask Q3. My advice is to never say anything negative about yourself in an interview. Ever. If asked this question, reply that there are no " difficult" customers but some are a little more "demanding " than others and you see that as a challenge and an opportunity to use more of your people skills. Say that you have **never** failed to deal with a customer to their satisfaction. Never say anything negative about yourself . Ever. Either in an interview situation or even when you talk to yourself every day, as we all do.   If asked question 3, give an example of how you successfully handled a demanding customer.

At this point it is necessary to point out that the wording of a question can vary greatly. The same question can be asked in many different ways and you must be very awake and sharp in an interview situation to realise this. I'll say more about this later.

4.3   The competency ' *Communication* ' can generate many questions, depending on the job. Naturally, there is a great overlap between *Communication* skills and *Customer Service* skills. These are all interpersonal skills.

The most frequently asked questions by interviewers on **Communication** are

Give me an example of when you :

1.   Communicated something difficult to someone. / Presented something clearly.

2.   Adapted your communication style to suit the listener / audience.

3.   Had to communicate something with sensitivity and tact.

From the advert, it's fair to expect Q1 to be asked, because we are, after all, trying for a job in a call centre ! Next, since the advert states that you would be writing 'customer-focused letters ', I would very much expect Q2 to be asked.

Next, we concluded that the competencies of **Attention to Detail** and *Negotiation* / Persuasion would arise. So, a question such as "*Give me an example of when you have had to work with great accuracy* " or "*Tell me of a time when you had to work with great attention to detail* " can be expected for this job. You will need really good examples of meticulous work to high standards. If you have had a financial background or even counted money on a till, you will need to show that you worked to zero tolerance. You prided yourself on your till always being penny-perfect when you handed over to your colleague. This might have only been a Saturday job long ago.

4.4   Similarly, since the advert stated that you must "promote services", you could easily be asked one of the most common questions of the **Negotiation - Persuasion** competency category Tell me about a time when you :

1.   Successfully negotiated something.

2.   Motivated someone to do something and how you overcame their objections.

3.   Argued your case for something and how you won it.

4.   Persuaded someone to buy something or do something.

I would expect Qn 1 to be the most appropriate for this job.

It's always possible in a job such as this that the interviewer will ask a question about the candidate's ability to fit into a team . Unusually for a call-centre, teamwork has not been mentioned in the advert, Perhaps this call-centre is not open-plan and each worker is quite self-contained in his own pod for most of the day and has little interaction with colleagues. Nevertheless, I would always have an example of teamwork ready for the interview , such as one in response to " Give me an example of when you have worked well in / contributed well to a team "

The ability to multi-task was "preferred" but not essential. It could come up as a question. It is best to be prepared for it with an example of when you have done more than one job at once with no loss of quality. Mothers are experts at this.

To summarise then, the most likely questions that will asked for Example A are:

(a) Tell me a time when you have given great customer service / gone the extra mile for the customer . (b) Tell me time when you have handled a difficult customer who had a complaint. (c) Give an example of when you have had to explain something difficult to someone in a clear manner. (d) Tell me of when you have had to communicate your style to suit the customer. (e) Give me an example of when you persuaded someone to buy something.

4.5   Example B from Chap 3.

Re-read Example B from Chap 3 and our concluded competencies from the previous chapter.   The most common questions asked around *Deadlines / Targets / Achieving* are :

Give me an example of when you :

1.   Successfully met your targets within challenging deadlines.

2.   Failed to meet your targets. / Missed a deadline.

3.   Your greatest achievement.

Again, the wording used can differ slightly. It's clear that this is a very target-driven job, where the bonus is almost 25% of the basic wage. It is certain that one of the questions will be similar to Qn 1. The employer will want to hear an example of when the candidate has had to work to demanding targets and deadlines and how he achieved them. He could also very well ask Q2, since this is also very popular with interviewers. The candidate should never portray himself in a negative light. Ever. If he was ever in danger of missing a target or deadline, he can relate how he renegotiated the deadline or enlisted help from a colleague to achieve his target or that he never missed deadlines because he always had the foresight to have a contingency plan inbuilt into his schedule. You never miss deadlines. Do you understand ? You never ever say anything negative about yourself in an interview. Ever. Ever. Do you understand ? No exceptions. Ever.

Since he is entering customers' homes, he could well be asked one of the common **Customer Service** favourites :

Tell me of a time when you have :

1.   Given great customer service or gone the extra mile for a customer.

2.   Dealt with a difficult customer or handled a complaint.

3.   Failed to deal with an awkward customer.

In this job, he will be reading the gas and electricity meters of people so that they can receive bills for their usage. Nobody likes receiving bills , so he can expect a cool welcome. Occasionally he may even experience hostility. He is quite likely to be asked any of the above . If asked Q2 or Q3, he replies that there are no " difficult" customers but some are a little more demanding

25

than others and you see that as a challenge and an opportunity to use more of your people skills.. He has **never** failed to deal with a customer to their satisfaction. I would expect Q2 because the employer will know that the applicant will regularly have to deal will uncooperative customers and will want to know how he has dealt with that in the past.

We concluded that he would be asked about *Attention to detail* , so we would expect a question such as *"Give me an example of when you have had to work to great accuracy "* or *"Tell me of a time when you had to work with great attention to detail "*.

4.6 Finally, we noted that **Self-Motivation** was called for and so it is likely that the employer will ask him for an example of when he has motivated himself . The most common questions are :

Give me an example of when you :

1.   Have shown real drive and determination to succeed.

2.   Have motivated yourself .

3.   Recovered from a serious setback.

Here, since the applicant will be faced with customers being out when he calls and the need to nevertheless achieve daily targets, it will require constant motivation and drive and the likelihood is that he will be asked Q1 or possibly Q2 and he will need good examples of how he has kept himself motivated in frustrating circumstances.

Summary :

(a) Give me an example of when you successfully met your targets within challenging deadlines. (b) Tell me of a time when you failed to meet your target. (c) Tell me of a time when you dealt with a difficult customer. (d) Give me an example of when you have had to work with great attention to detail. (e) Give me an example of when you have shown real drive and determination to succeed.

4.7 Example C from Chap 3.

Re-read Example C from Chapter 3 carefully and the concluded competencies. The most frequently asked questions on **Teamwork** are :

Give me an example of when you :

1.   Worked well in a team. / Helped a team achieve its target.

2.   Had a problem with a team colleague.

3.   Resolved conflict within a team.

It is certain that the candidate would be asked **Q1** - " Worked within a team " and perhaps Q2 also but I would not rate this as a high probability.

The most frequently asked questions by interviewers on *Communication* are :

Give me an example of when you :

1.   Communicated something difficult to someone. / Presented something clearly.

2.   Adapted your communication style to suit the listener / audience.

3.   Had to communicate something with sensitivity and tact.

For this particular post, it clearly states that the candidate will need to report clearly and accurately both verbally and in writing.   Therefore **Q 1** will certainly be asked. He will be asked for an example of when he has either had to report in person to someone , relaying clear and exact messages or else when he has written reports .It is highly likely that Q3 could be asked , since this is a role which requires great tact. I would say that there is a possibility, though a lesser one, that Q2 will be asked.

The most frequently asked questions by interviewers on *Customer Service* are :   Tell me of a time when you have :

1.   Given great customer service or gone the extra mile for a customer.

2.   Dealt with a difficult customer or handled a complaint.

3.   Failed to deal with an awkward customer.

Any of these questions could be asked, since it is a customer-facing role. I would suggest that **Q2** is almost certain to be asked : " Dealt with a difficult customer " and possibly Q3 too. I think Q1 is less likely to be asked

because the role of a Prison Officer is not to ensure that a prisoner will "
Have a nice day ".

The most frequently asked questions on **Negotiation and Persuasion** are :
Tell me about a time when you :

Successfully negotiated something.

1.   Motivated someone to do something and how you overcame their
objections.

2.   Argued your case for something and how you won it.

3.   Persuaded someone to buy something or do something.

In a job such as this, the Prison Officers will always be faced with objections
and I think Q 2 is quite possible. Q1 is possible too. Since the prisoners have
very little bargaining power, I would not expect Q4 to arise. Summary of
likely questions :

(a) Give me an example of when you have worked well in a team.(b) Give me an example of when you have had to communicate / report something clearly and accurately. (c) Tell me about a time when you have had to communicate something with sensitivity and tact. (d) Tell me a time when you have dealt with a difficult customer. (e) Give me an example of when you have motivate someone to do something and how you overcame their objections. (f) Tell me about a time when you have persuaded someone to do something.

Chapter 5 How to answer competency questions

So, you have been through the advert with a fine toothcomb and concluded which competencies are required. Then, you again very carefully analysed it and have predicted some of the likely questions.

Your next step is to look through your Experiences Autobiography and find experiences which can be used as examples for your answers.

5.1 Recognizing that an experience can serve several masters

It's important to realize that an experience can be used to answer several competencies. Remember Josh (Chap. 2.2) who had to send that urgent fax ? He could use that experience to answer both a Problem-Solving question which was thrown at him or an Initiative question. If someone had worked on a helpdesk in a supermarket, answering customer enquiries, they could use that experience for any Customer Service, Problem-Solving, Communication or Teamwork question. If you had worked shifts on a till in a shop, you could use that as an example for Attention to Detail or Flexibility or Communication or Customer Service. If you had taken on that job after suffering a major setback in your life such as a bereavement or separation or illness, then you also use it for Drive or Determination or / Resilience or Self Motivation.. Be careful about using illness however, unless it was just an accident, as employers generally do not like to hear about illness.

5.2 Choosing your examples

Always try to choose an example which matches the job description as closely as possible. For example , you are trying for a job as a cashier in a super-market.

The advert demands that you have a great attention to detail. You have three examples of this. Firstly, you worked in a post room , weighing letters. Secondly you worked as a cashier in a betting-shop. Thirdly, you measured and cuts lots of material for your hobby of home-decorating.

It is best to use the example of your time as a cashier because this most closely resembles this job for which you are now applying. **Always try to choose an example which matches the job description as closely as possible.**

5.3 The question format

The interviewer will most often ask you to show your competency using one of the following phrases :

- Give me an example of when you ………………
- Tell me about a time when you ……………………
- Describe a situation in which you / Describe a situation when …….
- What has been your greatest / worst ………………?
- Have you ever ………?
- When did you …… ?

5.4 The S.A.R. answer format

The simplest way to answer the interviewer's questions is to use the **S.A.R format** to tell a small story which will last around three minutes on average. Using this small , simple format ensures that your story has a logical flow.

Firstly, you will set the scene by describing the **SITUATION**. This is telling the interviewer what the situation or problem was that needed your attention. It is putting things in context.

Next, you will describe what **ACTION** you took to remedy the problem. This is where you go into the specifics and spell out exactly what you did and it gives you the opportunity to sell yourself to the employer. This is where you demonstrate how you have the competency which is being sought in the job advert. You tell how you have already successfully dealt with this situation in the past. You must detail not only what action you took but what skills you employed. Wherever possible, try to choose an example which is similar to the job you are now applying for. Wherever possible, try to demonstrate that you have **already done** exactly what the interviewer is asking.

Finally, you summarise the **RESULT**, detailing the benefits to your past employer and team and if possible, with hard figures if you improved productivity or saved money. If you can't quantify the experience with figures, describe what you learned from it. Also, add any praise or awards you received.

Approximately 10 % of your time should be spent setting the scene, 75% describing the action that you took and 15% describing the result.

5.5 S.A.R or S.T.A.R ?

You may have seen the S.T.A.R model for answering questions, where S = Situation, T= Task, A=Action and R=Result. In this model, you are also asked to explain the task you faced. I recommend that you stay with the S.A.R model as it is simpler. Why complicate matters ?

5.6 Writing your scripts

You have identified experiences which you can use for your examples. Hopefully, you will have several for each competency. Don't panic if you have only one or none at this moment. Choose the strongest and most relevant example you have.

The next step is that you will write a script for yourself for each example, practise it and then use it at the interview.

When writing your script, you will need to consider the following :

Situation and task : What was the situation ? What was the task you faced ? What was the problem that needed solving ? How did you get to be given it ?

Action : What action did you take and why ? Were there several approaches you could have adopted ? If so, why did you elect to take the one you did ? What skills did you use which demonstrate the competency exactly ? Show the steps you took and any difficulties you faced. How did you overcome them ? If people resisted you, how did you counter their objections ? Include key indicator words which demonstrate the competency. These are provided for the most common competencies in Chapters 7 and 8.

Result : State how you completed the task and what you learned from it. State the benefits to the employer or the team or the customer. If you have improved productivity or saved money, **quantify it with hard figures** . Don't say " I made my company a lot of money. ". Instead, say " I increased turnover by 5%, which equated to £20,000 per year." Or, " I saved my employer 7% on his stationery charges, which equated to £800 per year". Then maybe quote any praise or positive feedback you received from a customer or your Team Leader or any bonus or rewards.

5.7 You are expected to boast !

In our normal life, we are taught not to boast . It is frowned upon and we isolate people who do. However, there is one exception in life when boasting is not only acceptable but expected and that is in an interview. You must absolutely tell the interviewer how capable you are because you only have this one opportunity. He is not a mind reader. He cannot know your abilities You must spell them out for him.   Be proud of your skills and your achievements.   Yes, you are allowed to boast in an interview **but boast about your skills and achievements, <u>not about YOU</u>**. Say that you are proud of having achieved XYZ , not because you are brilliant but because you worked extremely hard or you made many sacrifices or overcame many obstacles to get it. I want you right now to change your mindset about any reservation or shyness you have about boasting. Believe me - it is expected in an interview. Don't let that precious opportunity pass you by. It might not come again.

Example 1   *"Give me an example of when you have been adaptable to change "*

Now for an example. Mark has read a job advert. It states twice that he must be adaptable to change and so he is expecting to be asked for an example of this. He looks through his Experiences Autobiography and he finds an example of when he worked for local government in the public transport section and when he was suddenly told that he would have to work in the Information Unit the following week to cover sickness absence. He had only ever been shown around there once before and knew that there was IT and switchboard which was unfamiliar to him .

He knew none of the staff and knew that the place was manically busy. His usual job was giving out info to the public face-to-face but he was suddenly going to have to adapt to working in a very busy call-centre environment , something he had never done before.

The challenge for Mark now is to script this in a way that he will be able to demonstrate his competency in the best way. He will write his script and probably change it a few times until he is happy with it. . He will read it to friends and family and get their feedback. Maybe he will record himself on

32

tape or into his computer or phone to hear how he comes across and to time himself. He will practise, practise, practise.

Answer :

"Yes, I worked in local government in the Transport Department. Normally, my job was working in the shop selling all sorts of transport tickets to the public and answering their enquiries on the routes of buses, trains, ferries and the underground . But one Thursday, my Team Leader told me that the following week, I would be needed in the Information Unit because several staff there had gone down with a virus.

It was a call-centre environment there and they worked on a very large switchboard that I was unfamiliar with and they had other IT and telephony that I hadn't used before too.

So, the first thing I did was I adopted a positive approach to the change, seeing it as an opportunity to learn more skills and more efficient working practices and maybe add something to my CV. The second thing I did was to start to manage the change instead of becoming a victim of it. I planned a visit. I asked my Team Leader if I could spend some time the next day, the Friday, at the Information Unit, familiarising myself with the equipment and acquainting myself with the staff and the layout of everything. She agreed to let me spend the Friday there.

So, I learned as much as I could before the big change. I'm really glad I made that plan because there was lots to learn. They liaised with many external partners such as the Police, Coastguard, Emergency Services, the Press, the utility companies etc. and I learned how to do that. I familiarised myself with as much of the tech as I possibly could and even the canteen, toilets and my own route there, so as minimize the strangeness the following week.

The result was that on the Monday morning, I hit the ground running. Those two weeks were extremely pressurised but because I had planned the change and managed it, it had been a disruption to me but not an upheaval. I had learned new switchboard skills too , which I added to my CV. The Team Leader of the Information Unit was so impressed with my work after that fortnight that he asked me to join his team permanently. I had decided to be the manager of the change, not its victim ."

He used **some** of the all-important **competency indicators of Change** ... *I adopted a positive approach.....I saw it as an opportunity to learn more skills ...I planned the change...I made full use of new tech .....I managed the change*

From Chapter 7, you can see that I have listed key indicators of the Adapting to Change competency. He used some words which all demonstrate that he was adaptable and flexible to the process of change. He managed and planned his two week disruption in advance, rather than reacting to it.

When you compose any script, you will be aiming to include some key indicators of the competency in it.

Notice that Mark *explained the background to the story*. He explained how things were before the change.

Notice how he has spent *most of his script describing the action that he took* : He adopted a positive approach.... He managed the change.... He asked his Team Leader ...He familiarised himself with as much as he could in advance .

Notice that *he used* " *I* " throughout the narrative.

Notice that *he explained what he had learned and how he had benefited* from the experience. He ended the story powerfully, both in saying that the Unit's Team Leader tried to headhunt him and also repeating a memorable slogan. ...manager of the change, not the victim.

5.8   Using effective, descriptive action words

When writing your scripts, it is important to use specific, descriptive **action words** which tell the employer exactly what you did. It is not enough to keep saying " I did this and then I did that and then I did something else."

If you are giving an example of ' Attention to Detail ', it sounds far better to say " I carefully **monitored** the dials" rather than " I checked the dials." If you were answering an ' Initiative ' question, it's better to say that you **"pre-empted** a potentially serious accident in the workplace " rather than you stopped someone slipping on water. When giving an example of ' Problem Solving' and telling how , while resolving the problem, you noticed part of the procedure was no longer necessary so you **streamlined** it. That sounds much better than " I cut parts out ". Employers like to hear " streamlined", since it suggests a saving of their money. You will find a list of action words to use in Chapter 9. Add your own words to the list as you go along but a word of warning : make sure you know the correct meaning of a word before using it. Use the words for accuracy, not for ego.

5.9   Keep your scripts

When you are happy with your script, having perhaps have tried it out in front of family or friends, put it in your Experiences Autobiography. Hopefully, it will help you to land this job and then you will not need again for a long time but do keep it, to save you having to write it again.

5.10 Teamwork example

This time, here is an example in which the interviewer is asking about Teamwork :

Example 2 " *Tell me about a time when you have worked well in a team* ".

Answer :   **"Yes, there was a time when the council was selling off all the houses on the estate to a Housing Association and it invited the tenants to form a tenants' association. I became a member of the team, which comprised of 20 members. There were many issues to be discussed - such as whether the high-rise blocks were to be demolished or not and there were different groups of people with different agendas and fears. The team itself was quite diverse so it was going to be a real challenge to get everyone to work together.**

One of the first things I did was to promote equality and diversity by ensuring that the pensioners and teenagers got just as much speaking

35

time as everyone else. Over the course of the six months that I was a member, I respected and valued the diverse views, perspectives and experience of all the other members. Whenever I gave feedback about their suggestions, it was always gentle and positive. Similarly, I respected and accepted the feedback from fellow team-members about my suggestions. I acted as one of the main liaison points between the team and all external interested parties , such as the Police, Social Services, Probation, etc.

I contributed to the team with my ideas and I contributed to the team morale with humour and enthusiasm. I resolved disputes and conflict among team-members by finding common ground and seeing that contradictory views are sometimes misunderstandings or misinformation. I shared my ideas and knowledge with the team. I treated everyone with respect at all times. I compromised over decisions and put the common group goal above my own.

The result was that the estate was transferred over to the Housing Association and I facilitated in playing a part in ensuring that everyone had a say in the process. I had helped several diverse groups to work together as a team. I had gained valuable experience from liaison with several agencies , which later stood me in good stead in terms of references for jobs."

Notice that he set the scene and explained that there were diverse people with different agendas

Notice that the bulk of the script is taken up with the Action that he took ... I promoted...I respected...I gave ....I acted....I contributed.........I resolved......etc.

Notice that he included **some** all-important **competency indicators of Teamwork** : *I promoted equality and diversity........I respected diverse views, perspectives and experience.......I gave gentle, positive feedback........I respected and accepted feedback.....I contributed my ideas.......I resolved disputes ....I shared my ideas and knowledge ....I treated everyone with respect ......I contributed to the team morale with humour or enthusiasm ....I compromised ....I helped*

These are all words which tell the interviewer that he is an excellent team-worker. It could also be used as an example of Diversity.

5.11 Checking your script

You will not get your script right the first time and will have to amend it several times before you are happy with it. Use this checklist as a guide :

- Is most of it taken up by the action part of what you actually did ?

- Have you included everything ?

- Have you repeated yourself by accident ?

- Have you mostly spoken about what **you** did in the " action " part ?

- Have you chosen an example which is similar to the job you are now applying for ?

- Have you described the benefits to you or the team or company or customer and if appropriate, been able to **quantify** them with hard figures and percentages ?

- Have you said what you learned and/ how you have grown from the experience ?

- Have you **finished with a strong impact** , that the employer will remember ?

5.12 Match your example to the job

When you look through your Autobiography, it is important to always use an experience which matches the duties of the job you are now applying for as closely as possible. For example, let us imagine that you are told to give an example of a time you have delivered great customer service. If you have 7 or 8 examples of when you have given great customer service and the job you are now going for is in a call-centre requiring some sales or persuasion, look for which one your examples where you have given great customer service whilst also persuading someone.

Similarly, if the job description mentions a requirement for problem-solving, use one of your customer service examples where you also solved a problem for the customer. In other words, don't just select any old example from your lists. Carefully select which of your experiences is best suited to the job you are now applying for. The more examples you build up, the easier this becomes.

5.13 If you can't think of any examples

If you have really spent time looking back at all the experiences in your life, both in work and outside, as I have described in chapter 2 and you have looked at the examples given under the competencies in chapters 7 and 8 and you still can't think of any examples of things you have done which match the competencies in the job advert, then I would suggest that the job may not right for you. Listen to your heart. It is the best guide. Unless you are reaching out for a radically different change of career, it seems that you could well be going for a job that might be unsuitable for you. Are you sure you want to do this ? You can never be happy unless you are true to yourself. Follow your own inner nature, no matter what. There are too many square pegs in round holes. You will never be happy in life until you find the right hole for yourself.

5.14 If you can't memorise your scripts

You must practise your scripts after you have decided on the final draft and are happy with it. Then you must practise again and again. Some people have used a tape-recorder or mobile-phone to record themselves speaking their example and then playing it back again and again until they know it off by heart, almost like a pop song.

However, if you feel that your script is fine for an application form but that you have the memory of a goldfish and are unable to remember the whole script, you can either write a much shorter script or else just note down key points. Pick the bones out of them.

In either case, it is vital that you stay with the S.A.R format and also that you mention a few key indicators of the competency.

Chapter 6 : What to do and what NOT to do

Guidelines for answering competency questions :

THINGS YOU MUST DO :

- ✓ Use examples can be from any area of your life.
- ✓ Have more than one example prepared for each competency
- ✓ Try to choose an example which matches the duties in the job description as much as possible
- ✓ Talk in specifics about what you did, relating your skills to the competency and to THIS job, if possible.
- ✓ Talk about what **YOU** did, not what the team did.
- ✓ Detail **HOW** you achieved it.
- ✓ Don't spend too much time setting the scene.
- ✓ Convey as much information in the shortest possible time, emphasising key skills.
- ✓ **Quantify** your success, if appropriate, with figures and stats. If not, say you were praised by someone.
- ✓ Boast about your skills, <u>not about you</u>. Say your achievements are due to hard work and sacrifice, just as much as your skills.
- ✓ Stay focused on the question.
- ✓ Ensure your example has a happy ending !
- ✓ Finish with a **strong impact** and with you being praised, if that's appropriate.
- ✓ Practice your scripts in front of friends or family , if possibleWhen you are writing your scripts, don't fall into any of these traps:

Things you must __NOT__ do :

x   **Don't assume** the employer knows the background. Carefully set the context.

x   **Don't generalise** : eg "I'm always polite to customers .. " - The employer is not interested in how you normally are. He wants an example of what you have <u>done</u> <u>already</u> which shows that skill.

x   **Don't give a job description** : eg "My job involves..or   I do this ......" The employers is not interested in what your job involves. He wants an example of what you've <u>done</u>.

x   **Don't theorize** : eg "Well, I would do/ I generally/ I tend to ." The employer is not interested in what you <u>would</u> do. He wants an example of what you have <u>done</u> in the past which demonstrates that particular competency.

x   **Don't assert** : eg   " It is very important to get along with your colleagues ". The employer is not interested in your assertions. He wants to hear an example of when you have <u>done</u> which shows that particular ability.

x   **Don't depersonalise it** : eg   " <u>We</u> decided to ..." Say what **YOU** did, not what others did .**Use " I ",** not   " We ".

x   **Don't blind him with science** : He might not know the technicalities of your job.   Keep it simple.

x   **Don't use jargon**, abbreviations or slang. Don't assume the employer will understand your private language.

x   **Don't be unbalanced.**   Remember : most of the time should be spent on the Action section of S.A.R.

x   **Don't malign anyone.** Don't criticize customers, employers or colleagues.

x   **Don't use controversial subjects**. Stay with safe topics.

x   **Don't come across as Superman** : the examples don't have to be extraordinary . Just come across as being very good at your job.

•   **Don't talk for too long !**   Be concise and crisp. Don't beat about the bush.

Chapter 7

7.1   Adapting to Change Competencies

The interviewer wants to know how you have coped with sudden change, that you had a positive attitude towards it and that you adapted to new working methods. How you have improvised. How you do stuff which is extra to your job description.

- You took a positive "can do " approach to change, seeing it as opportunity to learn skills
- You were flexible, enthusiastic and open to new ideas
- You were willing to adapt to develop new skills
- You supported and made full use of new technology
- You kept yourself up-to-date with new technology
- You kept calm, didn't panic in changing circumstances
- You adapted your routine when there was sudden change
- You adjusted positively to rapidly changing priorities and simultaneous demands.
- You adapted your behaviour to new working practices
- You adapted your work to cope with changing priorities
- Your learned from your experiences and those of others and you adjusted accordingly
- You changed your behaviour as a result of feedback
- You multi-tasked, playing several different roles
- You revised your plans, decisions and working methods in the light of new information
- You were flexible when faced with unexpected obstacles and delays
- You worked effectively in situations of ambiguity and uncertainty
- You always managed the change, rather than becoming a victim of it

Adapting to Change Examples :

✓   You adapted to a new boss or teacher or colleague.
✓   You transferred to a new site or shop or location.
✓   You were asked to take on new tasks and responsibilities.
✓   You learned new software or technology or equipment.
✓   You retrained or went on a course.
✓   You had your shift pattern suddenly altered.
✓   You were suddenly caught up in an unexpected fire, disturbance or crisis.
✓   You lost your job but adapted.
✓   You had to go part-time or job-share.

✓   You had to move home and settle into a new environment

✓   You adapted to a changing situation

✓   You reacted appropriately to an unexpected situation

✓   You raised kids - that certainly involved adapting to sudden changes !

✓   You volunteered to change shifts or holidays to help someone out

✓   You adapted to new technology at home - a new type of phone/computer/ modem or a new software system at work

Example "*Tell me of a time when you have been adaptable to sudden change*"

Answer :

" When I worked as a secretary, I had arranged the monthly meeting at the office for the managers in our area. That morning when I arrived in work, we found that there was rain coming in through the roof of the conference room. This was only about three hours before the meeting was due to start.

So, I adopted a positive approach and stayed calm. I checked to see if any other rooms could possibly be used but none could. I then quickly phoned each manager's secretary and told them not to let their manager set off until I had found a new location.

Since my manager was off, I took the initiative. I adjusted to the rapidly changing situation by researching local hotels and chose one which was highly recommended by a variety of sources for its high standards of service. I phoned it and booked a room there. I also booked some refreshments. I took the opportunity to have them to send details of their services. I then contacted the secretaries again with the precise details of the new location and arranged for the meeting to begin a little later in order to allow everyone sufficient time to arrive.

The result was that the meeting went ahead successfully. Since midweek rates were very cheap and he could network, the regional manager was very impressed and decided to hold all future meetings there. "

Notice how she included **some** competency **indicators of Adapting to Change** : *I adopted a positive approach ....I stayed calm...... I adjusted to the rapidly changing situation by .....*

✓ You planned a church fete. That day, there were rain and gales forecast, so rather than cancelling it, you improvised and moved it into the church hall.

✓ You planned you child's birthday party in the garden but when the weather suddenly turned bad, you adapted by moving it indoors.

✓ You were doing one job and were suddenly asked to do another job. So, you delegated some of your work or asked a colleague to take some of your tasks in return for a future favour.

✓ Two staff suddenly left in one week. So, you readjusted your shifts and also volunteered to do extra hours until a new worker started. Emphasise that you worked smarter as well as simply doing extra hours.

✓ You worked in the storeroom of a shoe shop and were told that in two weeks' time, you would have to work on the till. You adopted a positive approach and asked if you could spend 10 minutes of your lunch observing the till cashiers at work, since you knew nothing about debit cards, etc. That was agreed. When you began your till training, it was so much easier.

7.2 Attention to Detail Competencies

The interviewer wants to be sure that you have a keen eye for detail, that you paid great attention to your work and that you controlled your errors.

- I double-checked the accuracy of my work using a structured checklist
- I had someone else check my work, if appropriate
- I measured everything at least twice. - " Measure twice, cut once."
- I was careful, meticulous and thorough
- I continually sought to improve my accuracy
- I took pride in my work
- I had a zero tolerance policy to my own mistakes
- I prevented distractions to my work
- I took a ' Right-First-Time ' approach to my work
- I kept all relevant data, calendars, schedules handy
- I ensured data and equipment was updated regularly
- I took any important messages in writing
- I had any messages and numbers repeated and unusual names spelled out
- I followed all procedures and standards

Attention to Detail Examples :

- ✓ You worked on a till or did the petty cash.
- ✓ You worked with figures a lot.
- ✓ You carefully measured or weighed or calculated things. You fitted carpets. You measured wallpaper.
- ✓ You measured tiles. You cut lengths of valuable materials.
- ✓ You monitored instruments, dials, meters or gauges.
- ✓ You checked, inspected, did quality control.
- ✓ You copied or recorded details perfectly.
- ✓ You entered data onto a spreadsheet or template or database.
- ✓ You copied and scanned important legal documents or similar financial ones.
- ✓ You arranged items, such as a collection of books/CDs in alphabetical order.

45

✓ You catalogued items meticulously and re-checked.

✓ You filed papers or books in strict order to specified rules.

✓ You processed information / data in order to balance the equation/ books.

✓ You made a meticulous record of things.

✓ You did stock ordering or stock control.

✓ You followed very strict guidelines, rules or procedures to the letter.

> ✓ You took the minutes of your team meetings. You then checked the accuracy. You then emailed them to all who attended for review and further thoughts to be signed off as a true record. When done, you forwarded them to all relevant absentees and partners.

> ✓ John gave an example of how he worked in a call-centre which took emergency calls from people reporting gas leaks. He told how he had to enter names, totally accurate addresses including postcodes and totally accurate phone numbers. He then had to give out accurate instructions to the caller. He then had to despatch the emergency gas workers. He included getting the caller to repeat the address and phone numbers back to him and spell any unusual names. He was commended each year for his accuracy.

✓ You worked in a Customer Services Department in an office and you noticed that many of the problems revolved around the staff recording the customers' emails slightly incorrectly : the letter O was often transcribed as the figure zero and the letter I was being written as the figure one. You suggested that every use the same phonetic alphabet. It was agreed and adopted.

✓ You were awarded 'Best in Shop for Till Management.' You were always penny perfect.

✓ You had computer programming as a hobby : so, if you typed even one comma or full stop (period) incorrectly, the program wouldn't run, so attention to detail was crucial.

7.3   Communication Competencies

The interviewer wants to be sure that you understood that communication is a two-way process, the importance of active listening, the need to check your understanding and the need to speak in a structured manner.

- You actively listened, giving your undivided attention - not interrupting, pre-judging or assuming
- You established rapport and personalised the encounter, using their name, not account number
- You asked open and probing questions to gain info and understand needs and issues
- You explained why information was required
- You explained complex processes in a simple manner
- You used clear, concise, unambiguous language, avoiding jargon or slang
- You presented information in a structured, logical format and in context
- You pitched your language, content and style at the appropriate level for the listener
- You were positive and polite at all times
- You paused to allow him to contribute
- You checked your own and others' understanding
- You confirmed his understanding via questioning
- You summarised your points to ensure clarity and mutual understanding
- You kept focused on the issue in question
- You gave praise, thanks and constructive feedback
- You conveyed disappointing news with tact & sensitivity
- You shared ideas, information and feedback
- You relayed relevant info to those needing to know it
- You provided knowledgeable and credible responses to queries

PHONE SKILLS : All the above plus :

- You were prepared with pen, paper & PC switched on
- You had all your necessary information at hand
- You were not eating, drinking or chewing
- You answered promptly, within two rings
- You answered with a smile, enthusiasm and warmth
- You gave a greeting and identified yourself
- You did not speak too quickly
- You considered time differences of the caller
- You considered possible disabilities of the caller
- You actively listened
- You individualised the call, using caller's name
- You empathised, if appropriate
- You apologised, if appropriate
- You use appropriate questions open, closed, probing
- You had caller spell out unusual names
- You checked the message you had taken
- If transferring, you first ensured contact was available
- If transferring, you explained to caller the reason and contact's name
- If putting on hold, you asked caller's permission
- You checker your understanding by short paraphrasing
- You followed up on any actions you promised to caller

WRITTEN COMMUNICATION : all the above   PLUS

- You used a variety of illustrations (charts, graphs) to explain your points, if appropriate
- You used correct grammar, punctuation and spelling
- You organised your ideas clearly
- You wrote in a brief, clear, logical and well-structured manner using appropriate style
- You provided examples and comparisons , if appropriate
- You checked communications have been received and understood
- You chose the right method of communication (email / letter / text / etc to address the recipient

FACE-TO-FACE : all the above PLUS

- You watched for non-verbal clues / body language and responded appropriately
- You responded with non-verbal actions (nods and smiles) to show your understanding
- You used a variety of media and graphic aids to reinforce your points and maintain interest

Communication Examples :

✓ You explained something to an elderly person or a young child - how to use a PC, camera / phone.

✓ You explained something complicated to a new work colleague, customer / neighbour. A rota /roster. Timetable. Application-form. Test. Notice. Letter.

✓ You gave a message to the public, perhaps over the tannoy.

✓ You wrote a procedure guide for new members of staff.

✓ You listened to a customer who had a complaint.

✓ You took a message carefully and relayed it.

✓ You wrote an important email or letter.

✓ You gave a talk or presentation to a group.

✓ You answered the phone.

✓ You explained procedures to a new work colleague.

✓ You met and greeted someone.

✓ You took messages on a reception desk

✓ You designed an advert or poster or flyer to announce or sell something.

✓ You gave a speech - perhaps a best man speech.

✓ You sold stuff at car-boot sale / garage sale /shop /market stall /fete

✓ You interviewed people

✓ You befriended the elderly or needy in a food bank

✓ You helped kids to read

✓ You took phone-calls from vulnerable students

✓ You took part in the debating society

✓ You acted in the drama group

✓ You presented a show in the hospital or student radio

✓ You were a member of the local residents' association or homewatch group

✓ You participated in a Parent - Teacher forum

Example   " Give me an example of when you have communicated something clearly to someone."

Answer   "At the Careers Office, I had to give a talk to a class at the neighbouring college about our services. My task was to deliver a professional talk that was informative , accurate, interesting and relevant.

Since we talk differently to people of different ages and backgrounds, I prepared by investigating my target audience by phoning the college tutor to find the make-up of the class : their age-group, course and aspirations. I also asked her what she thought they would wish to gain from my talk.

I then considered my style of communication (simple but not condescending) , my content and my presentation (whether to use PowerPoint, video, flipcharts, etc.). Finding that the class would consist of 20 students, I suggested to my manager that a short video followed by a 10-15 minute talk by me, using one or two flipcharts to illustrate our procedures, followed by a Question and Answer session would be the best schedule. She agreed.

I explained to the class what we would do because communication is always more successful when people know in advance what will happen. While speaking, I used vocabulary which was appropriate to that age and client group. I avoided using jargon, abbreviations or slang that they would not know. To maintain interest, I used various techniques : I used humour; I paced my speech with pauses, knowing that people have different attention spans; and I alternated my speech with the images on the flowcharts. To help them remember what I said, I used repetition, linking, reinforcement and summarization.

After checking everything had been understood correctly, I handed out leaflets for them to browse through and held a very lively Question and Answer session. The result of the talk was that the Q & A session was very lively and spontaneous, with the students wanting to know much more about our services. The other result was that the college tutor was so impressed that she arranged for the careers visits to become a regular feature at the college. "

Indicators of Communicating : *I investigated the target audience and its needs.....I considered my style, content and presentation .....I explained in advance what would happen .....I avoided jargon, abbreviations and slang....I paced my speech with pauses -I alternated my speech with images....To aid memory, I used repetition, linking, reinforcement and summarization....I checked understanding..*

Example   " Give me an example of when you have communicated something clearly to someone "

Answer :   " I had a Saturday job in a camera shop and quite often, we had customers in who just wanted a basic model but did not know how to operate it. Since I   explained complex things in a simple way, my colleagues would refer those customers to me for instructions, once they had paid for their cameras.

Firstly, I established rapport , by saying hello and giving my name and then put them at ease by telling them that digital cameras were much easier to use now than before.   When explaining, I used clear, concise and unambiguous language, pitching it appropriately for the listener and I avoided any technical jargon or slang.

After finding out their intended intentions, I explained how to navigate the different buttons, controls and menu system in a gentle, logical and structured way , taking into account their attention spans. I checked their understanding by asking questions and also by watching for non-verbal clues such as puzzlement . I summarized my points and helped them to remember things by repetition, linking and summarization. I then invited them to try the controls themselves, if they wished to do so.

The result was that the customers said time and again that I had made the whole process so easy and quick to understand. My colleagues and Team Leader were very happy because they could get on with selling more. "

Indicators of Communication : - explained complex things in a simple way .- established rapport - I used concise, unambiguous language - I pitched it appropriately - avoided any jargon or slang - .I explained in a logical &structured way - took into account attention spans - checked understanding with questions and looking for non-verbal clues…I summarized my points.

7.4 Customer Service Competencies

The interviewer is looking to see that you displayed the range of interpersonal skills needed to service customers with excellence : including active listening, transparency, checking mutual understanding, balancing of needs, managing expectations, over-delivering and taking responsibility for the whole enquiry / complaint/ transaction. " Going the extra mile" (doing more than the minimum).

- You established rapport and personalised the encounter, using their name, not number
- You cleverly established the customer's hierarchy of needs with suitable questioning
- You actively listened - not interrupting, pre-judging or assuming
- You checked your understanding of customer's situation and needs by paraphrasing or summarizing
- You empathized with the customer's situation
- You communicated clearly, avoiding jargon, slang and abbreviations, so as not to confuse him.
- You pitched your language, content and style at the appropriate level for the listener
- You considered any special needs such as age, disability, health, cultural background or language
- You presented him with a range of appropriate options and alternatives
- You tactfully balanced his needs with the business needs
- You was honest and transparent as to our policies
- You managed his unrealistic expectations
- You protected the customer's security, confidentiality and privacy
- You remained patient, helpful, professional and polite at all times
- You were positive at all times and conveyed bad news with sensitivity
- You sought assistance if you were unable to resolve the immediate problem
- You explained your processes and time-scales to avoid call-backs

- You continually updated yourself with the latest policies, products
- You delivered excellent customer service by being an expert at your job
- You ensured the customer was happy with the resolution
- You took responsibility for the customer's problem or complaint or wishes
- You solicited the customer's level of satisfaction at the end of the encounter
- You followed up on actions that you had promised or on his enquiries
- You considered how feedback and complaints could improve your service
- You under-promised , then over-delivered
- You went the extra mile
- You gave a customised service, not lip-service
- You aimed for a 'Right-First-Time' approach when dealing with customers

Customer Service Examples

- ✓ You worked in a shop or a market stall
- ✓ You worked in a call centre
- ✓ You worked on a helpdesk
- ✓ You worked in the library for two weeks as work experience
- ✓ You worked as an unpaid volunteer in a charity shop
- ✓ You worked weekends or during the summer holidays in your uncle's shop
- ✓ You helped out at your local school or church fete
- ✓ You held your own jumble sales, garage sales or yard sales
- ✓ You manned the phones at charity begathons
- ✓ You handled complaints. You dealt with demanding, irate customers
- ✓ You gave someone a lift. You went the extra mile in some way for someone

Example   " *Give an example of when you have given excellent Customer Service"*

Answer :   "When I worked in a shop, I was deputising for the manager one Saturday. The security guard came over with an old woman who said she had put her bag down and someone had stolen it. She was crying, very distressed and frightened .

I took her into the office, established rapport with her by asking her name and giving mine, sat her down and asked her if she would like a cup of tea. I got the security guard to rustle one up for up for her. I got all the relevant info from her by getting her to tell me exactly what had happened. I actively listened, by not interrupting , judging or assuming anything. I empathized with her , saying the shock must have been awful and I checked my understanding as to what had happened.

I took into consideration her special needs : she was hard of hearing and elderly and so I spoke clearly, slowly and loudly. I explained our processes and asked her if she wanted to involve the Police, which she did. I called the Police and before they took her home, I asked if there was anything else we could do for her. We had no CCTV at that time. Thankfully, her keys were not in her bag and I asked her if I could call on her after work to check that she was okay.   That afternoon, I organised a collection for her from the neighbouring shops in our mall and raised twice as much as the money that she had in her bag. I called on her later that day with a colleague and she was overjoyed.

The result was that she became a regular customer and told all her friends about what we had done for her. The story actually made the local paper. We gained about 5% new customers after that good publicity. I recommended to my manager that we get CCTV and she arranged it ."

Note how she included **some** of the all-important competency **indicators of Customer Service** ... *I established rapport... I gathered all the relevant info....I actively listened by not interrupting, judging or assuming anything ....I empathized....I checked my understanding......I took into consideration her special needs ....I explained our processes....I asked if there was anything else we could do for her ....*

Notice that she went the extra mile by organizing a collection and calling in on her. Notice too that she quantified the success by giving a %.

Example   " *Give me an example of when you have resolved a customer's complaint or handle an irate customer. "*

Answer : " When I was working in an electricals shop, a woman came in who was very angry complaining that a washing-machine she had bought from us had broken down again after only two weeks.

I let her vent, not taking things personally and then empathised, saying it must have been very frustrating for her. I apologised for what had happened and then I established all the facts by effectively questioning her. I actively listened, by not interrupting or judging or assuming. She said it had broken down twice already. I checked my understanding by paraphrasing.

I reminded myself not to argue or be defensive. I remembered that we had already had several complaints over that model . I asked her what she wanted the outcome to be and I tactfully balanced her needs with the business needs by explaining to her what we could and couldn't do : we to replace it with a new one, her money to be refunded or for it to be mended again with a reduction on her payments. She wanted to buy a slightly more expensive model made by a different manufacturer. I explained the situation to my Team Leader and suggested that considering the circumstances, as a goodwill gesture, we allow her to exchange her machine.

He agreed. I checked that the customer understood and was happy with the proposal and for installation the next day. I put it in writing , we all signed up and I arranged the delivery and installation. We had a letter a month later from her saying she was thrilled with her new washing-machine. "

Notice how he included **some** all-important competency **indicators of Customer Service** : *I let her vent ... I empathised .. I apologised...I established all the facts by effective questioning ....I actively listened..... I checked my understanding by paraphrasing ... I reminded myself not to argue or be defensive .... I asked her what she wanted the outcome to be ..... I tactfully balanced the customer's needs with the business needs......I checked that the customer understood and was happy .... I put it in writing.............*

✓   When a customer came into my shop and his size of shoe was not available, I phoned a neighbouring branch, who had his size in. Since the customer was a tourist who didn't know our town, I volunteered to walk there to get it for him. I went the extra mile. Well, quarter-mile !

✓   You worked in an optician's. You went out of your way to drop off a pair of glasses at a customer's house on your way home from work, so that her young daughter could have her glasses for her exam in school the next morning.

✓   You were a taxi-driver. You took a family to an airport. You made a 10 mile return journey, at no extra charge, to collect a child's teddy bear she had left at the hotel.

✓   An irate customer phoned complaining his order had still not arrived. You investigated and found that his address had been incorrectly recorded and so the order had been returned. You took his correct details and got permission from your Team Leader to arrange a 25% discount as an apology.

7.5   Deadlines and Targets Competencies

The interviewer needs to know you understood the importance of planning, prioritizing and building in contingency time. He wants to know the lengths you went to, to achieve your targets and meet your deadlines.

- You queried the deadline
- You renegotiated and extended / re-scheduled the deadline
- You planned your objectives using the SMARTER model (Specific, Measurable, Realistic, Timebound, Evaluated, Re-Evaluated)
- You prioritized the tasks into Urgent, Important and Non-Urgent
- You built in some contingency time to allow for delays and unknowns
- You set your deadline earlier than the real one, building in overrun and checking time
- You enlisted help from colleagues and friends in exchange for future return favours
- You carefully delegated some work to others, if necessary
- You monitored your progress and objectives
- You used To-Do lists, diaries, calendars and alarms
- You used a Brought/ Forward system, if necessary, to ensure nothing was missed
- You usefully employed downtime such as waiting time, travel times etc.
- You worked overtime / came in early/ stayed late / worked weekends.
- You worked at home, if that was needed, to meet your targets or deadlines
- You focused on the desired outcomes
- You used the most suitable methods to get the job done

Deadlines and Targets Examples

✓   You completed work by a certain time.

✓   You submitted an essay or coursework by a certain date.

✓   You completed work for a customer by a set time.

✓   You repaired or serviced a car or machine for a customer for a set date.

✓   You prepared a report for a meeting.

✓   You met your sales targets in order to receive your commission or pay.

✓   You paid your bills on time.

✓   You learned your lines for a play

✓   You learned a piece of music for a recital.

✓   You organised a function, kids' party, a wedding, fete or a funeral

✓   You worked late or through your lunch or at weekends to meet your deadlines.

✓   Frank had a small company of computer programmers. They were planning to launch a new game when they read that a competitor was about to bring out a similar one just before their own. Frank decided to ask his team if they would postpone their holidays and all work longer to get the project completed ahead of schedule. They did and became a better team because of it.

Example   *"Give me an example of when you have had to work to a deadline"*

Answer: "A couple of years ago, I had the sudden offer of a job which would mean moving from my flat within 7 days. It was a case of move or lose the job. The problem was that my flat was full of all my treasured belongings - many books, CDs and lots of furniture, which I had to pack or sell off. It meant hard decisions and a lot of work within a tight deadline.

The first thing I did was I queried the deadline because often deadlines are not set in stone. I renegotiated it and had it extended by a further 2 days. I analysed all my jobs that lay ahead and the time and the resources I had available. I would have to contact all the utility companies, the council, the doctor, my landlord, the Royal Mail, the removal company and host of other parties too. I then planned my objectives using the SMARTER model (i.e. ensuring my objectives were Specific, Measurable, Achievable, Realistic, Timebound, Evaluated and Re-evaluated).

After spending some time thinking about how to prioritize all the tasks, I prioritized them into Urgent, Important and Non-urgent. I estimated a certain amount of time per task but I also built in contingency time to allow for delays and unknowns. I enlisted help from friends , who helped after work and all day on moving day and I carefully delegated appropriate tasks to them. I kept monitoring the work's progress and objectives on a daily basis using a B/F system in my diary and later on an hourly basis. I sold half my stuff and packed half.

The result was that I managed to move house in time. I had one or two very small minor breakages but I learned from experience. I donated a lot of old stuff to charity shops too. The whole experience reinforced for me the necessity of good planning."

Note how he included **some** of the all-important competency **indicators of Deadlines** : *I queried the deadline....I renegotiated and extended the deadline......I planned my objectives using the SMARTER model (Specific, Measurable, Achievable, Realistic, Timebound, Evaluated and Re-evaluated).....I prioritized into Urgent, Important and Non-Urgent ....I built contingency time ...I enlisted help from .....I carefully delegated.....I monitored the work's progress and objectives......I used a B/F (brought-forward) system.*

7.6 Decision Making Competencies

The interviewer needs to see that you followed an excellent decision-making model to identify your objective, gather relevant info, evaluate it, generate viable options, critically evaluate the pros, cons and risks and made a good decision.

- You identified your specific objective
- You identified your specific needs
- You collected as much relevant information as possible, from a wide variety of sources
- You ensured your sources were reputable
- You sorted the relevant from the irrelevant, important from the unimportant
- You ensured your data was current
- You organised the material in a way that aided analysis and extracted it appropriately
- You identified gaps, inconsistencies and links in the information
- You critically appraised the evidence
- You generated realistic options and discarded unrealistic ones
- You filtered the options into a shortlist
- You assessed the pros and cons and the risks of each remaining option
- You confirmed your understanding
- You knew your limitations and involved others with relevant expertise, if necessary
- You made your objective and impartial decision
- You evaluated your decision and confirmed/revised it
- You re-evaluated your decision and amended it, if needed
- You introduced quality assurance checks, where appropriate.

Decision Making Examples

✓   You decided to buy any expensive item, such as a house or car or TV.

✓   You had to decide whether to buy or rent a home.

✓   You decided which school to send your children to.

✓   You had to decide which hospital to go to.

✓   You had to decide which insurance plan / policy to take out or renew.

✓   You had to decide between several job offers.

✓   You had to decided between several financial investments / savings.

✓   You decided which contractor to hire for a job

✓   You had to make a decision over which university/course to attend.

✓   You had to decide whether to emigrate or not.

✓   You had to decide to relocate or not.

✓   You had to decide between various offers, such as bank loans.

✓   You had to decide between a number of job offers

Example   *"Give me an example of when you have had to make a major decision."*

Answer :   "A while back, although I had access to a computer at work, I realised that I needed a computer at home . I wasn't sure whether to buy a PC or a laptop. It was a major expenditure and since I couldn't afford to make a mistake, I had to ensure that I made the right decision.

The first thing I did was I identified my specific objective (buy a computer) and my specific needs - immediate, medium and long term. I asked myself how I would use it mostly. - writing ? Music ? family webchats ? How much speed and storage would I need and how soon it would be obsolete. I then collected as much relevant information as I needed from a wide variety of sources, ensuring the info was up-to-date (brochures in shops, websites, chatrooms, consumer groups, independent reviews). I then consulted with computer-shop assistants, friends and work colleagues for advice.

After organising the material in a way that would help analysis and extracting the relevant info appropriately, I generated realistic options for my budget, which led me to decide on a laptop. I filtered the options to a shortlist of three (based on spec, length of guarantee, IT support and price). After assessing the pros and cons and risks of each and confirming my understanding (by emailing the companies), I then made my decision.

The outcome was that I bought a laptop which served my needs perfectly. I never regretted my decision once and later saw that model go on to win many awards. "

> Notice that he included the all-important competency **indicators of Decision Making** and these must **always** be stated **in the correct order**
> ....*I .identified my specific objective and needs.....I collected as much relevant information as needed ...from a wide variety of sources..... ensuring it was up-to-date....I consulted for advice ..... I organised the material in a way that would help analysis and extracted it appropriately....I generated realistic options.....I filtered the options to a shortlist...I assessed the pros and cons and risks of each option   I confirmed my understanding.   I made my decision.   (This decision-making model should be used for any* decision you have made. In your example, you may need to add that you evaluated and then later re-evaluated your decision as you worked, but it wasn't appropriate here.)

✓   You received some money in a will and wanted to invest it. You researched all the bank & building society accounts, online and off and other options such as Premium Bonds, Fixed Rate Bonds, etc. You evaluated the pros, cons and risks of all of them. (Refer to key indicators).

62

7.7 Drive, Determination or Resilience Competencies

The interviewer wants to hear how you kept going despite many resistance or obstacles. How you persevered. How you recovered from a setback.

• **You adopted a positive and thankful approach**

• **You used the " SMARTER " goal-setting technique - Specific,Measurable,Achievable,Realistic, Timebound, Evaluated, re-Evaluated**

• **You broke the task down into small, bite-size chunks**

• **You rewarded myself after completing each small unit**

• **You surrounded myself with motivational quotes and family photos**

• **You prevented interruptions**

• **You prevented procrastination**

Drive, Determination or Resilience Examples :

✓   You recovered from a bad accident - maybe you learned to walk again.
✓   You recovered from a messy, long divorce
✓   You recovered from a protracted legal matter
✓   You recovered from a redundancy
✓   You recovered from bankruptcy
✓   You recovered from a devastating bereavement
✓   You finally had a baby after a very long course of IVF treatment
✓   You traced your family tree
✓   You tracked down someone , perhaps your real parent- after much work
✓   You passed your exams despite missing some time due to illness
✓   You fought a campaign and won
✓   You did not give up on something - you gave up smoking or lost weight.
✓   You had been out of work for a long time and were looking for shop work. There was not much of it about but you persevered by dropping your CV personally in every shop in a 4 mile radius , every 4 weeks until you were successful.
✓   You relocated to find work.

7.8 Equality and Diversity Competencies

The interviewer wants to be sure you were comfortable working with people from a range of diverse backgrounds and abilities.

- You treated everyone with respect and dignity

- You respected all differences in race, gender, age, ethnic background, sexual orientation, disabilities, carer levels and opinions

- You watched your own stereotypical responses and prejudices

- You learned about the customs and norms of others

- You took an interest in the background of others

- You were open and willing to listen to other viewpoints

- You promoted inclusion by supporting initiatives and programs to increase understanding of diversity

- You enrolled on equality and diversity courses, such as the Disability Discrimination Acts and Equality in the Workplace.

- You avoided making assumptions based on his accent or appearance

Equality & Diversity Examples :

✓   You volunteered to go on Equality/Diversity courses.

✓   You mixed with diverse races at school or uni or at work or in the block or street where you live.

✓   You learned the culture of your ethnic neighbours.

✓   You included the ethnic neighbours' kids in your kids' games and vice-versa.

✓   You suggested an interpreter service at work

✓   You looked after your disabled colleague when the fire-alarms went off.

✓   Fred told how he saw the two sons of his recently arrived Iraqi refugee neighbour always watching his sons' team play football but never being invited to play. He got the team to let the boys play and to find out about their life in Iraq and their customs. He met the parents, did the same, became good friends and learned so much.

✓   When you worked on your uncle's market stall, you took things from the back of the tables to the front so that disabled people in wheelchairs could more easily see and handle them.

✓   When you noticed your wheelchair-bound customers struggle after they had crossed the road and approached your shop, you asked the council to lower the kerb in front of your shop.

Chapter 8

8.1   Initiative Competencies

The interviewer wants to see if you had to be told to act when you saw a problem. He wants to know if you have ever had any ideas to improve methods . He wants to see if you just sat around waiting to be told what to do.

- You sought additional challenges and responsibilities, doing more than the minimum

- You anticipated and predicted customer needs

- You pre-empted potential problems by anticipating them

- You took appropriate action before being forced by circumstances.

- You acted quickly in a crisis

- You generated new ideas, suggested new innovations before being asked

- You designed new ideas, systems, templates for improvement

- You recognized and took advantage of opportunities to improve your company's productivity

Initiative Examples :

✓   You recognized opportunities, seized them and used them to your advantage..

✓   You saw a chance to save your company money/ increase sales or cut waste.

✓   You volunteered for extra work, when the company was struggling.

✓   You noticed a potential problem, maybe a health and safety issue and took action to prevent an accident before it occurred . Wet floor ? Dangerous mat or lead ?

✓   You foresaw potential difficulties and took pre-emptive action in time.

✓   You noticed a recurring problem & acted before being asked to remedy it.

✓   You acted quickly in a crisis, such as when someone was hurt in work, you were the one to call the doctor or administer First Aid or similar.

✓   You took the initiative to improve your company's working practices, perhaps by submitting a suggestion / inventing something/ redesigning something.

✓   You anticipated a customer's needs. A customer bought a garden patio from you and you suggested that he might want to also buy sunblinds. He did.

✓   You started your own business.

Example " *Give me an example of when you showed initiative.* "

Answer :   " While I was on my month's induction course at my new job with the Tax Office, I realised that MS Outlook would be used extensively and to a sophisticated level. Although I had used email before, such as Yahoo, I did not have those skills and I was going to need them every day .

So, I took the initiative and I asked for training in Outlook. To my surprise, this was refused due to lack of resources. I immediately looked for any online training modules on the inhouse intranet system , found some and asked the IT staff to set me up but was refused on the grounds that I was not to be given full access until my induction was complete. I would be under enough pressure dealing with the public, handling new software, new systems in a new job , with targets without having to stumble through an email system .I wanted to deliver a speedy, high-class service.

I took the initiative again by buying a Teach Yourself Outlook manual and learning the course at the library. I also updated my Windows knowledge and other MS programs skills to deliver the best performance possible. I then had my training assessed and certified.

The result was that my initiative had meant that I hit the ground running, delivered a first class-service, gained new certificates and was even being asked by colleagues who had started the same day for help. "

✓   Paul worked in an office. He noticed that the customers were often forgetting to sign their forms or enclose their money. He suggested the office redesigned the flap of the envelopes which they sent out , so that they were printed with the words " Have you signed your form and enclosed your remittance ?" in bold, letters where they could not be missed. His idea saved hundreds of man hours each month.

✓   Tom worked in the warehouse / storeroom. He noticed that the delivery notes had a superfluous page at the end. It had the company's details on and nothing else. He calculated that it came to a few thousand sheets of wasted paper a year at his location alone. He suggested a redesign of the form. It was adopted nationwide and saved the company £ 300 per year in stationery.

Example "*Tell me of a time when you used your initiative*"

Answer :   " I had just started in a new job and they did their post manually. After weighing and franking everything, they entered the details into a postbook. One day, when I needed to find something about a Special Delivery postage, while I was online, I happened to notice that we could do our posting online via the Royal Mail site and save a considerable amount of money, £60 per week to be exact.

I took the initiative to read more about it and then to phone them up for more details. I then wrote a short proposal to my manager explaining the situation and outlined how much we were currently paying by posting manually and how much we would save by posting using the Royal Mail online service. I explained that as well as being cheaper, it would also be quicker. I also explained that we could easily print off the details and that he could easily analyse posting costs and volumes at any time via our account.

He objected that we would be in a fix if our IT ever went down and were unable to send our mail, which absolutely had to go out that day. When I reassured him that I had already enquired about that scenario and been told that under those circumstances we could revert back to using our book, providing we attached an explanatory message on the slip, all would be fine. He agreed and told me to set up our account.

The result was that I saved our company over £ 3000 every year and more in man-hours, I was awarded an accolade for my initiative, which was a cash prize of £ 200. "

8.2 Integrity Competencies

The interviewer wants to know if you fulfilled your obligations and promises, were utterly honest and above board in all your dealings, treated everyone fairly and consistently and were beyond corruption. You did what was right.

- You were always honest and open and respectful
- You only ever made realistic, achievable promises and you fulfilled them
- You ensured confidential info remained confidential
- You refrained from gossip and spreading rumours
- You took responsibility for my own actions
- You fulfilled my work commitments
- You behaved ethically and professionally
- You applied all rules fairly
- You behaved consistently
- You were vigilant of all security policies and risks
- You ensured consistency between your communication and your actions
- You knew your limits and sought help when necessary
- You adhered to the organisation's policies

Integrity Examples :

✓ Joe told of the time of when he worked for the council planning committee and how one day after work, he was approached by a member of the public who tried to bribe him to allow his home extension. He did the right thing by reporting the incident to his superior the next day.

✓ You were in a shop and you were mistakenly given too much change from a £ 20 note. You told the cashier that you had only given her a £ 5 note, instead of dishonestly keeping the money.

✓ In work, you were told some cruel gossip. You never spread that gossip or confidential information. It later turned out to be untrue and malicious anyway.

✓ You always applied rules fairly, even when pressurised - You refereed a game.

✓ You kept confidential info away from people who tried to access it , such as payroll, marketing people or partners of battered wives trying to intimidate them.

✓ You resisted bribes for granting favours and for inside information.

✓ You kept your word at all times and moved heaven and earth to fulfil your promises. You worked weekends to keep your word.

8.3 Leadership Competencies

The interviewer is looking for evidence that you have led and inspired others by your professionalism, integrity, courage, enthusiasm, fairness, inclusiveness and insistence on quality.

- You accepted responsibility when no one else would
- You courageously stepped up to the mark in time of need
- You were a role model by your behaviour : always calm, polite, honest, respectful at all times
- You gained trust from others by being trustworthy, keeping promises
- You maintained strict confidentiality at all times
- You encouraged diversity and used its strengths
- You resolved conflicts among colleagues and customers
- You fostered teamwork by encouraging and rewarding cooperation
- You inspired and motivated colleagues by coaching / mentoring them towards their self-development goals
- You led with enthusiasm and personal example, mucking in myself
- You took decisive action
- You were alert to potential risks and problems, either in safety or reputation terms
- You delivered, demanded and assisted colleagues to deliver high quality output / service at all times
- You continually sought to improve yourself and the team
- You continually sought to cut waste

Leadership Examples :

✓ After hearing a colleague maligning the company to a customer, you stressed the importance of company reputation and got to the bottom of the colleague's discontent. You saved your company's reputation from further harm.

✓ When the Team Leader was off sick, you stepped in when no one else would to organise a quick, collaborative meeting in which you all eventually agreed on work duties. You had taken responsibility and gained cooperation of others. You had efficiently organised the whole team's workload for the day by your action.

✓ There was an ongoing conflict within your team , which was having an insidious and demoralising effect on everyone. The Team Leader knew about it but seemed unwilling or unable to resolve it and let it drift. You quietly stepped in and resolved it by finding common ground objectives.

✓ When the Area Manager confided in you about concerns and pleaded with you to be frank, you expressed your frustration that your reported concerns about the lack of quality control on your section were not being addressed. He said that he had been unhappy about your manager for a long time and was unaware about that and he made the necessary changes.

8.4 Managing Myself Competencies

The interviewer is looking for evidence that you are your own harshest critic, that you adopt Kaizen, which means constantly looking to improve the efficiency, quality and methods of your work.

- You took responsibility for your performance and targets
- You reviewed and evaluated your work regularly
- You sought and made use of feedback
- You maintained steady performance
- You sought help with excessive work pressure, if needed
- You remained focused on your objectives
- You prioritized your objectives and schedules
- You understood your development needs and sought ways to improve and to expand skills
- You learned from your experiences
- You learned from others
- You took responsibility for developing yourself and your career
- You motivated yourself to achieve the required outcomes
- You looked for opportunities to develop your role
- You stretched yourself
- You knew the status of your work at all times

Managing Myself Examples :

✓   You planned part-time study and childcare around your part-time job

✓   You raised kids while holding down a job !

✓   You planned and prioritized your family's resources within a very tight budget

✓   You joined evening classes / weekend classes to improve your skills

✓   You bought some online courses to improve your skills

✓   You taught yourself a new skill or updated your skill via Skype or Youtube

You can also use some of the 'Initiative ' competency examples for 'Managing Myself'

8.5 Negotiation Competencies

The interviewer wants to see that you have negotiated, not simply threatened to walk away if your demand was unmet. He wants to hear that you prepared, exchanged views, explored compromises, searched for possible solutions and common ground and found a mutually acceptable agreement.

- You prepared yourself in advance & clarified objectives
- You decided your bottom line in advance
- You prepared how to put your case and gave thought to his likely objectives
- You took a colleague for moral support
- You adopted a positive, polite, professional, collaborative , problem-solving approach
- You explained your view and then let him do most of the talking, to understand his position better
- You actively listened, not interrupting, pre-judging or assuming anything
- You watched his body language to read his attitudes, expressions and intentions
- You corrected any incorrect statements or omissions or faulty logic with polite questions
- You adjourned to consider his new proposals, if that was necessary
- You looked for a compromise, if needed, by exploring possible solutions
- You encouraged him to discover and embrace alternative perspectives
- You searched for common ground and looked for a win-win situation : the mutual saving of time, costs or waste and the potential mutual achievement of targets
- You were willing to make concessions, if needed, providing they were matched by similar ones in return
- You helped him to recognise the benefits of your concessions
- You secured a satisfactory agreement
- You had the detailed agreement put in writing
- You ensured the agreement included a detailed action plan which of its implementation

Negotiation Examples :

✓   You negotiated your own salary or pay rise.
✓   You negotiated your rent.
✓   You negotiated a contract for work you did or for a job you needed doing for you.
✓   You negotiated the sale of a large item - a house or car or similar
✓   You negotiated a series of lessons or a course.
✓   You haggled over something
✓   You bartered your services- you fixed their computer, they did your garden.
✓   You resolved a dispute between people by acting as a negotiator.

Example " *Give me an example of when you have negotiated"*.

Answer : " I needed to part exchange my car for a smaller one and saw an advert in the paper offering free road tax for a year as part of the deal on new cars. The ad was for a garage which sold a car I had been researching for weeks.

First of all, I prepared myself by checking the Motorist's Guide to see my car's worth, decided my bottom line and how best to put my case. I took the ad and took a friend for moral support.

At the showroom, I found the model , I explained my situation briefly and let the salesman do most of the talking. When he asked me what part exchange value I wanted, I invited him to make an offer instead. After he examined my car and offered £4,500 , I replied that it was worth at least £6000 because of its condition, regular service history and very low mileage and that I was looking for more than that. I confronted him with the Motorists Guide and my service history.

After he had upped his offer to £ 6000 but refused to go higher, I looked for compromise by exploring possible solutions. I searched for common ground and looked for a win-win situation . I offered to praise him to his HQ for his great customer service , to praise the showroom on several social media sites and drive around with sticker adverts on my car advertising his garage for 6 months. In return, I wanted free servicing for three years, free fog lamps and free air-conditioning.

After consulting with his boss, he returned and said I could have two of the three and they liked the social media idea a lot. I agreed. He said I drove a really hard bargain and jokingly said not to come again.

I got the detailed agreement in writing and was I more than happy with the outcome."

Notice how he used **some** all-important competency **indicators of Negotiation** : ...*I prepared myself.....I decided my bottom line ...I prepared how to put my case....I explained , then let him do most of the talking ....I looked for compromise by exploring possible solutions...I searched for common ground and looked for a win-win situation.......I got the detailed agreement put in writing.......*

8.6 Persuasion Competencies

The interviewer is looking to see if you have persuaded someone to do something by overcoming their resistance and objections. Perhaps how you have encouraged or motivated someone.

- You researched him, his intentions and objectives.
- You established rapport, mirrored his words & posture
- You took an interest in him
- You made him laugh, endearing him to you
- You flattered him but was careful not to overdo it
- You explained all the benefits and advantages to him
- You used comparisons, examples and stories
- You apologised, making you seem reasonable and honest
- You used repetition
- You urged him not to delay ... he'd miss the opportunity
- You offered him an elite, exclusive lifestyle that others will envy
- You offered him the chance to be fashionable, in with the in-crowd, a fashion icon
- You offered him something that would make him happy or look younger or sexier or work less or feel free or have more time or money
- You anticipated his resistance and objections
- You introduced peer pressure, telling him all his friends do it or have one
- You used one of his friends or family members to persuade him or confirm
- You told him   " You know you want to "
- You encouraged him to imagine the improvements or how good he would feel
- You told him " You will change your mind. It's inevitable ."
- You extinguished his objections, one by one
- You told him you could see he was already being persuaded
- You supported your points with logic
- You made him feel he was getting something rare
- You quoted the authority of others to support your claims
- **You assured him that he had made the right decision**
- **You facilitated his change**

80

Persuasion Examples :

✓   You persuaded someone to buy something from you.
✓   You persuaded someone to buy something for you.
✓   You got someone to do something for you, who really didn't want to do it.
✓   You got your kids to tidy their rooms
✓   You persuaded your boss to give you a pay rise
✓   You persuaded a colleague to swap his holiday for you.
✓   You persuaded someone to change job or house
✓   You persuaded him his friends were bad for him
✓   You persuaded someone to give up drink / drugs / cigarettes / overeating.
✓   You persuaded someone not to commit suicide.
✓   You persuaded someone to donate money.
✓   You persuaded someone to play for your team
✓   You persuaded someone to volunteer a few hours of their time.
✓   You used to run a teenage boys' football team. At first, you couldn't get them to arrive half an hour early for some pre-match practice. When you said there were lots of free sausage rolls for those who came early, they soon conformed.

Example   " *Tell me of a time when you persuaded someone to do something.* "

Answer :

" My friend had smoked for years and had tried to give up but failed. I started to notice that he was coughing quite a bit. He had already told me that he was spending a fortune on his cigarettes and I was concerned for his health so I decided to try to persuade him to give them up for good.

At first, I started by joking a few times that he sounded like an old man ready for the knacker's yard with that cough. I knew suggesting a visit to the doctor would be futile and he laughed it off. We were good enough friends for me to say that I knew he was spending £60 a week on cigarettes and that I knew a way of both cutting that down to £15 and stopping that bad cough of his. His ears pricked up at the amount he could save and I told him about some e-cigarettes that I had read about.

At first he was apprehensive and scornful, saying they weren't the real thing . I explained that they still had nicotine but reduced amounts so it was healthier. Knowing he liked to be in with the in crowd, I said it's now the fashion. I said I know a place where you can try before you buy and asked if I drove him there, would he try them. He agreed. He was amazed that they came in different flavours too.

The result was that he went onto e-cigs and saved himself a lot of money. More importantly, he took my advice to see a doctor and kept himself healthier."

Notice how he included **some** all-important competency **indicators** of **Persuasion** :
He used humour....... He explained the economic and health advantages to him......He appealed to his friend's herd instinct....He explained he could "try before you buy"....He facilitated the change by accompanying him and driving him there......

8.7   Problem Solving Competencies

The interviewer wants to hear how you solved a problem in a structured rather than a chaotic or lucky manner : how you defined a problem, analysed it and found the solution.

- You defined the problem as accurately as possible
- You identified the relevant info and organised it in a way to help the analysis
- You analysed the figures logically, using the 'W5H' model-(asking Who, What, Why, When, Where and How)
- You analysed the problem illogically ,laterally and from different angles
- You checked your assumptions
- You looked for the Point of Deviation from the normal system, step by step
- You identified implications, consequences or causal relationships
- You identified patterns or meaning from data or events not obviously identified
- You brainstormed
- You implemented the solution
- You monitored your solution to ensure the problem had been resolved
- You revised your solution, if necessary
- You took action to prevent the problem recurring

Problem Solving Examples :

✓   You fixed a faulty machine, that you had no idea what was wrong with at the start.

✓   You fixed a bike/motorbike/car/printer/till-roll.

✓   You fixed an annoying noise coming somewhere from your car. (No, not the backseat driver !)

✓   You debugged a piece of software code.

✓   You cured a computer virus on your PC.

✓   You had to fix an Excel spreadsheet but could not at first trace which formula or macro was faulty.

✓   You solved a DIY problem at home or on your car.

✓   You saw a recurring problem or hazard that you decided to fix.

✓   You were working in a very small shop which had a till that you had never seen before. The manager popped out, leaving you alone, the till roll started running out. You looked in the drawer underneath and found another roll but did not know how to change it. It was a really old, unusual type. You looked in the drawer for instructions but found none. So, you phoned the sister store and followed the instructions of their manager by phone.

Example *"Tell me of a time when you have had to solve a problem at work. "*

Answer : "When working on a helpdesk in a call-centre, our manager approached me , saying we had dramatically fallen behind our targets for calls answered. Our Team Leader was off sick so she told me to find out what the problem was. My task was to analyse the spreadsheet data for the last few months.

The first thing I did was to define the problem as accurately as possible : in this case, since I knew no one had been off sick, it was that our work was not being recorded accurately for some reason. After I identified the relevant info and organised it in a way to help analysis (breaking it down into months and printing it off), I couldn't see from the raw data what the problem was , so I broke it down further into its constituent parts (into each day).

I analysed our figures logically, using the familiar 'W5H model '(who, what, where, why, when and how) but had no joy. I then approached the problem illogically using lateral thinking and looking at it from different angles but still had no joy.

I checked my assumptions and asked myself "Am I assuming that everyone was entering the data correctly, even though they were experienced staff ? " Therefore, I looked for the 'Point of Deviation from the System' , step by step and then I found what the problem was - the number of calls recorded had dropped dramatically in the first few days of the New Year 2012 because some of the staff had been incorrectly entering the old year as 2011. They had been inserting the correct day and month but had still mentally been attuned to the 2011 and so the calls were being incorrectly totalled.

I suggested to my manager that we adopt a formula on the spreadsheet to write the date instead of manually typing it ourselves each morning and she agreed. The moral is perhaps not to take things at face value or make assumptions. "

8.8 Teamworking Competencies

The interviewer is trying to determine the ways in which you have contributed to the success of a team or whether you act selfishly.

- I was friendly, helpful and approachable
- I valued the diverse perspectives, skills, experience talents and needs of my colleagues
- I shared my ideas and relevant knowledge
- I showed interest in the opinions of others
- I placed the common group goal above my own goals
- I co-operated with customers, internal and external team members, stake-holders
- I pulled my weight in the team.
- I supported my colleagues with their workload, when I could
- I praised my colleagues when they were successful
- I sought opportunities for cross-functional working and collaboration
- I was flexible over shifts, duties and holidays
- I learned the role of others in the team, so as to work better together
- I accepted responsibility for my work
- I employed the diversity of the team to assist me
- I participated in team meetings and post-mortems
- I accepted feedback from colleagues on how I impacted on others
- I was always willing to compromise
- I treated all my colleagues with respect at all times
- I was patient, tolerant, didn't play the blame game or gossip
- I maintained team morale with positivity, enthusiasm and humour
- I offered only gentle constructive feedback
- I balanced my own needs with those of the team

Teamworking Examples :

✓   You worked in team
✓   You played in a sports team
✓   You worked on a project in school that required teamwork. Perhaps Geography or Science.
✓   You shared information with others in the team
✓   You offered to help others in the team when you had finished your work
✓   You improved team morale with humour
✓   You worked with neighbours to clear snow or litter
✓   You contributed to a team in your church
✓   You participated in a Parent-Teacher forum
✓   You worked in a team in your hobby group competing against other towns. Chess team ? Footy team ? Brass band ?   Choir ?
✓   You participated in a team when you were sent on a course
✓   You resolved conflict within a team
✓   You stayed longer after work to help a colleague
✓   You did more than your allocation of work
✓   You served on a jury
✓   You swapped your day off or holidays to help a team colleague
✓   You played in a band
✓   You showed flexibility over shifts

Example   " Tell me about a time when you worked in a team "….

Answer :   " Yes, there was a time when I was called upon to do jury service. The group was quite diverse in many ways . It ranged in ages from about 20 to about 65, from all socio-economic backgrounds, from various races, colour and religions. I thought it would be interesting to see if everyone would work together.

For my part, what I did was I respected and valued the diverse views, perspectives and experience of all the other members. Whenever I gave feedback about their suggestions and ideas , it was always gentle and positive. Similarly, I respected and accepted the feedback from fellow team-members about my suggestions and observations. I praised their good suggestions. I employed the diversity of the group to assist my understanding.

I contributed to the team by sharing my knowledge and ideas and I contributed to the team morale with humour and enthusiasm. We could not agree upon a unanimous verdict and so were ordered to reconsider . When we were still unable to reach a 10 to 2 verdict, were again told to go back until we did. By this stage, some tempers were getting frayed. Some people were just wanting to go home. I resolved disputes and conflict among team-members who argued, by finding common ground and seeing that contradictory views are sometimes just misunderstandings and misinformation. That helped and we finally reached a 10 to 2 majority verdict which the judge accepted.

The result was that I facilitated in playing a part in ensuring justice was done as much as possible. I had helped a diverse group to work together as a team. I had gained valuable experience from the event, by working with such a diverse group and it later stood me in good stead, as it helped me get a better job. "

He included **some** competency **indicators of Teamwork** : I respected and valued diverse views, of other s. I gave gentle and positive feedback....I praised their good suggestions....I employed the diversity of the group to assist me ...I contributed to the team by shared by knowledge and ideas ...I contributed to the team morale with humour and enthusiasm....I resolved disputes by finding common ground.

More Teamworking examples ......

✓ You informed your colleague, who had returned to work after a period of illness, of the new changes, procedures and modifications to the software interfaces, rather than see her struggle on her first days back. You prioritized the info, giving her only the most relevant material. She praised you to the Team Leader.

✓ At the food bank / neighbourhood watch scheme, you typed & printed the menu choices / minutes.

Chapter 9   Action Words to Use

When writing your scripts and when in the interview, use these words to describe the actions you took :

I achieved
I adapted
I adopted
I analysed
I arranged
I assessed
I built
I combined
I compiled
I completed
I conducted
I controlled
I considered
I consulted
I coordinated
I created
I delivered
I designed
I developed
I devised
I diagnosed
I directed
I eliminated
I enabled
I encouraged
I ensured
I established
I exceeded

I expanded
I extracted
I evaluated
I evolved
I fostered
I furthered
I gained
I gathered
I generated
I identified
I implemented
I improved
I initiated
I increased
I influenced
I instigated
I integrated
I introduced

I launched
I led
I liaised
I managed
I minimised
I monitored
I motivated
I negotiated
I offered
I organised
I perfected
I performed
I persevered
I persuaded
I planned
I pre-empted
I prepared
I prioritized
I produced
I progressed
I promoted
I proposed
I queried
I quantified
I raised
I recovered
I redesigned
I reorganised

I rescheduled
I resolved
I restored
I saved
I secured
I simplified
I solved
I streamlined
I strengthened
I suggested
I trained
I transformed
I volunteered

Chapter 10   The interview

10.1 There are bad interviewers   Be ready for bad interviewers. Some will constantly interrupt you while you are narrating your example but don't let that throw you. Stay calm. Be sure you can back up what you have said. They may probe you for more in-depth details or for clarification.

10.2 Recognizing the questions   Part of the skill in handling competency questions is recognizing what an interviewer actually wants from you. Thankfully, most questions will be straightforward. If an interviewer wishes to know how you have adapted to changes in working practices, he will usually say something like : *" We are a fast-moving environment here with many shifting demands and we expect our staff to be flexible to those demands. Can you give me an example of when you have had to cope with such changes ?"*

However, some questions will not be so clear cut . Their question will be indirect and oblique. If you are unsure in any way as to what you are being asked, it is **vital** that you ask. It is no use to anyone if you narrate a competency example which is not the one which was required.

10.3 They may take notes   One of the interviewers may well be taking notes as you answer. Don't be phased by this at all. In fact, see this in a very positive light : the more they write down, the more they like what they are hearing;   the more key indicators you can include in your story, the more you will be demonstrating that you meet the competency. If you see them taking <u>lots</u> of notes, it's a very good sign.

10.4 Silences and feedback   Expect silences from them but don't expect feedback. After you have given your example, sometimes there are awkward silences in an interview. Don't be tempted to waffle to fill the silence. Don't expect immediate feedback , either verbal or in the form of smiles or nods. However, don't worry about this. It's normal. Have faith. If you have prepared your examples well, you already have a massive advantage over those who have not bothered and there will be many like that.

10.5 You can refer to your notes   You can take your scripts to the interview as reminders but you can't read them all the way through ! The interviewers will not mind you glancing occasionally at bullet points or headings you have highlighted to remind yourself. Your interview is not a memory test and they will not expect you remember everything.

10.6 If you can't think of an example
If you struggle to remember an example, firstly, **play for time**. Ask the interviewer to give you a moment to think or ask if you can come back to that question later. That will not count against you

Secondly, realise that your experiences serve several masters and can be used for several competency answers. **Competencies overlap**. When you are delivering excellent customer service, you are also communicating well, so that could be used to answer two competency questions.

The example given for ' Adapting to Change in Chapter 5, could also be used for Initiative, if you were on the spot and could not think of anything. Examples for Communication can often be used for Customer Service and vice versa. An example given for Deadlines can often also be used as an example of Managing Yourself.

The example of Negotiation could be used for Persuasion, if you were really on the spot and could not think of any other example.

" **Tell me about your biggest achievement** " is a very common question. Don't be surprised if you get asked it. If you are, then your answer can come from any of these competencies : Deadlines and Targets, Drive, Determination . Resilience, Initiative, Negotiation or Problem Solving.

Thirdly, **use your imagination**. Remember your long-forgotten uncle who had a small business. Yes, him. I'm sure you can remember him if you want the job badly enough.

10.7 Appear natural
Although you will have rehearsed your stories many times, make it appear as though you have thought them up on the spot and not rehearsed them. You need to appear as though you are fully competent at your job and do it effortlessly.

10.8 Heed the usual interview protocols : Take yourself
there early. Check the location in advance using Google Maps or similar and the transport. Even make a dummy run. Arriving early will allow you some last-minute revision of your notes. Get there early and revise your CV and answers. It pays off.   **Take your smart clothes.** Dress smartly. If you are wearing something for the first time, such as a new shirt, wash it first

so that you feel comfortable in it.   **Take your scripts / notes and CV.**
…to look through beforehand.

Take the right attitude. If you had arranged to meet one of your friends in a coffee shop in town at the weekend, I bet you would be relaxed and confident. That's exactly the attitude you must take to the interview. Have the attitude : " *I am well prepared and I know that I am going to be offered this job. It is not really an interview,* **it's just a** <u>*chat*</u> *. Of course I will be offered the job !   I have put more work and preparation in than the other candidates. It's a mere formality.* **I'm not nervous because it's not an interview - it's a chat.** "

Many jobseekers have told me that the advice of seeing the meeting as a "<u>chat</u>" rather than an interview was really effective in dissolving their nervousness. They report that believing that they **already   had the job** gave them great confidence. Take the right attitude. Confident but not arrogant.

If you have prepared your examples and rehearsed them well, you will be raring to demonstrate them. Many other candidates just can't be bothered. You can. That's what makes the difference.

Chapter   11   " Competency Options" tests

The application process for certain jobs involves your having to complete a Competency Options test. In this, you are given a situation and told to rank four given responses which most closely matched the behaviour you exhibited in that situation.

  For example, in a Customer Services situation, you are told to think of a time when you dealt with a customer who was very demanding in terms of the time, advice and amount of help they wanted from you. You are told to rank these four responses in order from 1 to 4, with 1 being the response you took and 4 being the least likely you would have taken :

A … I began with the intention of treating everyone equally but I found that I liked some people more than others and I admit that I was more likely to help those more.

B ... I can't pretend that I treated everyone the same. The ones who were undeserving and had bad attitudes got the bare service from me.

C ... I tried to be always fair and helpful but I must admit that how I treated people varied with how they treated me and how I felt on the day.

D ... I ensured that I was as fair as could be and that everyone received the same treatment , no matter how I felt personally.

The best way to tackle these is to firstly look for the worst response : in other words, the response that you would certainly NOT have done and to mark it as number 4. So here, I think you will agree that the poorest example of delivering customer service is option B. Naturally, someone working in a customer service role cannot decide to give the " bare service" to their customers, just because the customers are being demanding   or " undeserving " !

The next step is to identify the response that you would have taken. Here, it is option D. So, you mark that as number 1. You gave your best service to every customer, regardless of how difficult and demanding they were.

That is the strategy that you must always adopt   : firstly identify the worst response because usually it is the easiest to decide and assign it to number 4.   Then secondly, identify the best response and assign it to number 1. The remaining two options usually have only a very subtle difference between them and it is not too important in which order you place these. I would assign the second best response to A and the third to C.   Final answer ....1-D, 2-A, 3-C, 4-B.

Another example ...You worked in a team and are told to rank these in order.

A ... When I worked with others, I valued the differences between us and that each person had something different to contribute.

B ... I found it difficult working with people who were different from me because you need people with more similarities than differences.

C ... I appreciate that people were entitled to be different from me and I tried to adjust to their different ways.

D ... I was quite uncomfortable if they were different from me and found it difficult to adjust to their different ways of thinking.

Again, follow the strategy .. look for the WORST option.......look for what you would NOT have done or said and mark that as number 4 ......

I think you will agree that the worst option has to be the last one . Now, look for the best one and mark it as number 1 .... I think you will agree that it has to be the first one in the list above : he " valued " the differences, whereas the third option only tried to adjust . I would now suggest that C is better than B and so C comes second..   Final answer = 1-A, 2-C,3-B, D-4.

Another example ....You had to maintain accuracy in your work.

A ... I didn't check my work, as people were generally satisfied with it.

B - I spent almost as much time checking my time as I did doing it.

C - I checked those parts where errors could most easily creep in.

D ... I always checked my work , though as I grew in experience and confidence, I was able to spend less and less time on this.

Following the strategy, you look for the worst option and assign it to number 4. Then find the best option, that is, the one that you actually did and assign that to option number 1. Then decide the better of the remaining two and assign it to number 2.

Final answer is 1-D, 2-C, 3-B, 4-A

A is clearly the worst. It shows idleness, complacency and arrogance. B is the next worst . At least this person checks their wok but the employer would not recruit someone so incompetent. Of the remaining two, C is the poorer because errors can creep into any area of our work, not just the parts we expect.

The clever way to tackle these is to do them with friends and to share your thoughts. Two heads are better than one and five heads are better than two.

Don't fuss too much about the inner answers. It is the first and last in the ranks that you must get right.

Finally, before you submit your answers, recheck that you have written them in the correct order. It is very easy to record them incorrectly.

Chapter 12 - After the interview and beyond

If you don't get that particular job

The secret in getting a good job is knowing the right thing to do, doing it and **persisting** in doing it until you are successful. When you have been rejected for a position, it can be for many reasons. You might have demonstrated your competencies perfectly but the employer felt that you would not fit into the culture of his company or that team for whatever reason. Sometimes, an employer will withdraw a vacancy after the interviews. It does happen . It could be that you were considered excellent but one candidate had slightly more experience than you. It is common for six candidates to be invited for an interview . Four might have scored less than 80 %. You might have scored 96 % but the winner scored 96.5%. Since you don't know how close you came to landing that job, you will feel that you are a failure and that you will never master these competency interviews and that you will never get the job you want. Sadly, this is what we tend to do. We think the worst. We catastrophise.

Examine how you performed and be honest. If you felt that you performed badly on any examples, ask yourself why. Did you need **better** examples ? Did you need **more** examples ?   Did you need more practice ? If you were prodded for more details, were you able to give the specific detail that was wanted ?

What is important is that you move on and persist.

By constructing an Experiences Autobiography, you are doing the right thing. By constructing and learning your scripts according to the model I have given, you are giving the employer examples of the key indicators of the competencies he is seeking. You are doing the right thing and on the right track. The final unit is for you to show perseverance. You will succeed if you persevere. The formula works and you will win when the conditions are right.

What also counts is the time and effort you have expended in remembering all your experiences. Go back through your Autobiography and cross-check it with the key indicators given in chapters 7 and 8 and examples suggested underneath them. If you have very few experiences and examples and are really desperate, think of experiences of your brothers and sisters and friends.

Keep updating your Experiences Autobiography

You must constantly keep adding to your Autobiography with examples of your behaviours. If you are currently working, stay alert to how you are contributing to your team for examples of Teamwork. If work in a Customer Services environment, record examples of how you have delivered excellent service and how maybe dealt with demanding customers and complaints. Simply spend 10 or 15 minutes at the end of each working day remembering what you did that day. It's easy if you travel by train or bus to jot it down in your diary or record it into your phone or mp3 voice recorder. Make it a daily habit of forcing yourself to briefly skim through all the competencies and note down any examples. Then some time later, you can expand them into scripts. *__I cannot emphasise this enough.__*

When you get the job - <u>and you will, sooner or later</u> ......

When you get that email or letter and you have calmed down after all the excitement, Congratulations !   Go out and buy yourself a treat ...... a nice cake or some sweets or a nice fruit drink !

I told you the formula works !   You will join the hundreds that I have already helped into work. All I ask is that you please email me on **yetanothersuccess@gmail.com** to tell me .

I promise never to share your email with anyone. Ever. I simply like to know how many people I have helped get a job and I like to hear what competency questions were actually asked. **It would be great if you could also share your own examples with me, if you wish. Thank you.**

Finally.......

If you bought this book on Amazon

If you have found this book helpful and you bought it on Amazon, please be so kind and give it a good rating. You might also wish to buy another copy to give to someone you know who is looking for work or to change their job.

If you are stuck for a present to buy someone, please buy them my book called **The Best Quotes to Help You through Life.** Maybe you know someone who has a birthday soon who would like it ? A Christmas present ?

My other book is out soon and is about how to write a CV / resume that will get you that all important interview. You can't demonstrate your great competencies unless you have an interview and sadly, many folk cannot write a CV which will get them an interview. My book will help you to do that . Please buy it from Amazon.

Thank you. I wish you all the luck and all good things in life.

Mike

NOTES

....

....

....

....

....

....

....

....

....

....

....

....

....

....

....

....

CPSIA information can be obtained at www.ICGtesting.com
Printed in the USA
LVOW11s1559200715

446912LV00016B/1020/P